Ultimate
Sports
CAR

Ultimate
Sports
CAR

Quentin Willson

DK

DK PUBLISHING

London, New York, Munich, Melbourne, and Delhi

Senior Editor Nicki Lampon
Senior Art Editor Kevin Ryan
DTP Designers Sonia Charbonnier, Rajen Shah
Production Mandy Inness
US Editor Margaret Parrish
Managing Editor Sharon Lucas
Managing Art Editor Marianne Markham
Category Publisher Stephanie Jackson
Art Director Carole Ash

Produced for Dorling Kindersley by
Phil Hunt Editorial and
Cobalt id
The Stables, Wood Farm
Deopham Road
Attleborough
Norfolk
NR17 1AJ

Designers Lloyd Tilbury and Paul Reid at Cobalt id

First American Edition, 2002
02 03 04 05 10 9 8 7 6 5 4 3 2 1

Published in the United States by
DK Publishing, Inc.
375 Hudson Street
New York, New York 10014

Copyright © 2002 Dorling Kindersley Ltd, London
Text copyright © 2002 Quentin Willson

DK Publishing offers special discounts for bulk purchases for sales
promotions or premiums. Specific, large-quantity needs can be met with
special editions, including personalized covers, excerpts of existing guides,
and corporate imprints.
For more information, contact Special Markets Department, DK Publishing,
Inc., 375 Hudson Street, New York, New York 10014 Fax: 212-689-5254.

A Cataloging-in-Publication record for this book is available
from the Library of Congress.

ISBN 0-7894-8945-7

Reproduction by Colourscan, Singapore
Printed and bound in Slovakia by Neografia

See our complete product line at
www.dk.com

CONTENTS

Introduction	6
The Forties	16
JAGUAR SS100	20
MG TC MIDGET	24
JAGUAR XK120	28
BMW 328	32
The Fifties	36
ASTON MARTIN DB3S	40
JAGUAR XKSS	44
JAGUAR C-TYPE	48
MORGAN PLUS FOUR	52
TRIUMPH TR2	56
CHEVROLET CORVETTE	60
LANCIA AURELIA B24 SPIDER	64

FORD THUNDERBIRD	68
ALFA ROMEO GIULIETTA SPIDER	72
MGA	76
MERCEDES 190SL	80
BMW 507	84
AC ACE-BRISTOL	88
AUSTIN-HEALEY FROGEYE SPRITE MKI	92
SUNBEAM ALPINE	96

The Sixties — 100

LOTUS SEVEN	104
PORSCHE 356B	108
DAIMLER SP250 DART	112
AUSTIN-HEALEY 3000	116
FACEL VEGA FACELLIA	120
JAGUAR E-TYPE	124
TRIUMPH SPITFIRE MK3	128
MGB	132
CHEVROLET CORVETTE STING RAY	136
MASERATI MISTRALE SPYDER	140
SUNBEAM TIGER	144
AC COBRA 427	148
DATSUN FAIRLADY 1600	152
AC 428	156

The Seventies — 160

ALFA ROMEO 1300 JUNIOR SPIDER	164
MORGAN PLUS EIGHT	168
TRIUMPH TR6	172
LOTUS ELAN SPRINT	176
TRIUMPH STAG	180
JAGUAR E-TYPE V12 ROADSTER	184
MERCEDES 280SL	188
JENSEN-HEALEY CONVERTIBLE	192

The Sports Car Revival — 196

PORSCHE 911	200
MAZDA MX-5	204
FERRARI F355 SPIDER	208
TVR GRIFFITH	212
MERCEDES 500SL	216

Index	220
Acknowledgments	223

INTRODUCTION

MG Midget ad

Trying to actually define what a sports car is feels a lot like wrestling with a mattress full of molasses. There simply is no dictionary definition. Yes, they're usually low, quick, and pretty. They're also drafty, damp, uncomfortable, and impractical. But must they be convertibles or hardtops, must they always have big engines and just two seats? Should they be capable of a minimum of 100 mph (161 km/h), and should they always handle better than sedans? An MG TC (see pages 24–27) is a sports car, but a Rolls-Royce Silver Shadow is quicker. A Sunbeam Alpine (see pages 96–99) is also a sporty two-seater, but one that could be out-handled by a Ford Escort twin-cam sedan. A Ferrari Daytona coupe should be called the King of Sports Cars, but it has a metal roof and two rear seats. As soon as you start laying down any kind of formal parameters to define this most emotional of cars you start to think of machines that have always been considered sports cars, but don't meet your new set of rules.

And you can't use shape as a criterion. A BMW 507 (see pages 84–87) is very much a sports car, but the similarly open-topped Ford Thunderbird softtop (see pages 68–71) definitely is not. You could say that handling, roadholding, crispness of response, and

Style over substance
The MG TC has the looks of a traditional sports car, yet doesn't have the performance capabilities of other sportsters.

sensuality of controls might be what distinguishes the sports car, but you'd be wrong. All these can be found in a BMW 3 Series, which is far less sporty than a Mercedes 280SL *(see pages 188–91)*, which feels downright soft. What about the racetrack? Should all sports cars be suitable for competition? If that's the case, what about sedans like Hudson Hornets, Chevy Impalas, and Ford Mustangs that dominated circuits in the '50s and '60s? But while not every sports car has a blue-chip competition heritage, the race circuit has played a huge role in the genesis of the genre – but we'll come on to that later on.

> "The race circuit has played a huge role in the genesis of the genre."

THE SPEED FACTOR

What about performance and power? Most people equate sports cars with speed, but if you expect a two-seat, droptop Mazda MX-5 *(see pages 204–07)* to beat a four-seater, metal-roofed Subaru Imprezza, you're going to be hugely disappointed. The same thing is true of the MGB *(see pages 132–35)* – arguably the quintessential sports car of the '60s and '70s, it simply runs out of steam at just 100 mph (161 km/h).

Early classic
BMW's 328 set the racing world on fire in the '30s with its good looks, technical ingenuity, and all-around flair.

A British definition of a sports car from around 1910 was anything that a gentleman could not enter without stooping or removing his hat. By the '30s it was considered to be a fast, handsome two-seater. In the '60s, an American journalist came up with the tongue-in-cheek description of any car in which the seats could be folded flat to make a double bed. While none of these efforts move us toward any formal definition, that last ironic one gets us closest. Sports cars should always be fun, individual, good-looking, fast, charismatic, but above all else, hugely emotional. We love them because they're a welcome antidote to workaday family sedans.

To really understand what a sports car is, though, we have go back to when the description was first coined, back to the '20s and '30s. Bugattis, Bentleys, and Alfa Romeos were street-legal versions of Grand Prix racers. They brought the sport of competition to ordinary owners. Carmakers soon realized that by making their road cars look like thinly veiled racers they could tap into a world of glamor, speed, and sexuality. The divine Bugatti Type 35 was a road car you could race on the weekend, as were the monster Bentleys of the '30s.

Race-winning performance and Grand Prix looks became very marketable commodities, which made

Beautiful Beemer
The BMW 507's supremely elegant design and vibrant engine encapsulated the essence of wind-in-your-hair sports car driving.

well-heeled owners seem rugged, exciting, and very desirable. Soon the entire auto industry realized that racing actually sold cars, and manufacturers spent mountains of cash supporting race teams. And they didn't always need to win. For the public just to see something screaming around a circuit that vaguely looked like the car they could buy from the showroom was enough. The sporting connection brought a halo of association to street-legal sports cars, and starry-eyed enthusiasts bought them with grateful enthusiasm.

And the simple principle of buying something that looked like a racer was how the reputations of icons like the BMW 328 *(see pages 32–35)* and Jaguar C-Type *(see pages 48–51)* were born. Both were hugely successful in competition, and both could be bought

> ## "Companies poured millions into their competition departments in the full knowledge that a presence on the racing circuit guaranteed sales."

straight off the showroom floor. Fast-forward to the '60s and we see how the European auto industry had turned the marketing of competition cars into a black art. Companies like BMC, Rootes, Jaguar, Mercedes, Triumph, Ferrari, and even humble Lotus poured millions into their competition departments in the full knowledge that a presence on the racing circuit guaranteed sales. The Rootes Group didn't sell many Sunbeam Tigers *(see pages 144–47)*, but by competing

1955 Ford Thunderbird

in events like the Monte Carlo Rally, the Tiger brought glamor to the Sunbeam brand and made the similarly styled, but much slower, Alpine sell in numbers.

POWER OF ASSOCIATION

In the '50s Jaguar spent millions on motorsports. In fact, the English company's reputation was built on the racetrack. Of all the facets of the Jaguar brand, winning races is still the strongest, which is why it's desperate to carve a niche in Formula 1 today. Everybody old enough remembers those epic battles between D-Types and C-Types and how those swoopy, racing green

The allure of the racer
Drivers such as Stirling Moss helped manufacturers like Jaguar promote its road cars on the back of racetrack successes.

projectiles dominated Le Mans throughout the '50s. In 1961 Jaguar rolled out its glorious E-Type *(see pages 124–27)* and, as normal, ensured that the E was seen on circuits all over the world. Images of lightweight Es tearing around tracks appeared in newspapers and on the new medium of television. But here's the point. Jaguar didn't need to campaign the E. By 1962 it could sell every one it built and more; the waiting list stretched to the horizon. They didn't need to race because they'd already cemented their reputation. The Jaguar E-Type had become the archetypal sports car, an icon before it was even unveiled.

Other manufacturers watched and sighed with admiration. Jaguar had pulled off an enormous marketing coup. Even if its products were never seen racing again, the Jaguar brand would forever be associated with sports performance. And that's why the '60s became *the* era for sports cars. Yes, the motor mandarins knew that hurling their dinky two-seaters around tarmac made them sell in decent numbers, but making and racing sports cars gave them an even greater bounty: it made their brand appear exciting and desirable. The sports car had become an enormously powerful marketing tool that made ordinary sedans with the same hood ornament appear powerfully alluring.

Rally exposure
The attraction of buying a race-tested car – this MGB secured a class win at the 1966 Targa Florio – helped the B to become the biggest selling single-model sports car ever.

RISE OF THE SPORTS SEDAN

The promise of performance became the marketing men's mantra. BMC plastered the MG logo on as many sedans as it could; Triumph tried to convince us that the 2000 was a sports machine; and even Ford hoped its GT40 would help sell ordinary cars like the Mustang. And it worked. The new wave of performance sedans traded on a direct connection with sports cars. Why suffer in a cramped two-seater when you could have a faster and better handling sedan? Then the market changed. The industry realized that sports cars were more expensive to make than hot sedans and sold in smaller numbers. The late '60s and '70s saw the status of the sports car start to wane.

The glamorous Sixties
Tony Curtis made a special visit to Jaguar's Brown's Lane plant in 1968 to pick up his Racing Green E-Type Roadster.

Competition benefits
Sunbeam did well with the Tiger, using its entry into high-profile races such as the Monte Carlo Rally as a springboard to promote less exciting models.

And then the genre of the sports car suffered an almost fatal blow. Safety legislation in the US ruled that open two-seaters were dangerous. Draconian crash regulations created huge financial and aesthetic problems for the sports car. The pretty MGB became encumbered with ugly cowcatcher rubber bumpers. So were the MG Midget and Austin-Healey Sprite *(see pages 92–95)*. Jaguar, BMC, and Triumph were faced

> ## "Draconian crash regulations created huge financial and aesthetic problems for the sports car."

with huge engineering costs and a sales decline in their most important market – the US. Slowly, open two-seaters were deleted from manufacturer's product lines. The blizzard of legislation from America coincided with a sea change in the public's attitude to

the idea of owning a quaint old convertible. Advanced engineering came to the fore, with sophisticated sedans becoming more fashionable.

A DIP IN FORTUNES

BMW created a huge new market with its 3 Series; Mercedes rolled out its sporty 190E; and Jaguar's XJ6 sedan outsold its convertible XJS by a factor of 20. The number of sports cars available in America could be counted on the fingers of one hand; and in Europe two-seaters became low volume, specialized cars made in tiny numbers. Now everybody wanted quick sedans, executive expresses, or hot hatches. The sports car had become passé, antiquated, and uncomfortable. Mercedes carried on with its exquisite SL convertibles, but they weren't really sports cars. Porsche did good business

Keeping it real
Unaffected by rules and regulations, the Lotus Seven was one of the few no-frills models available for the genuine sports enthusiast.

Federal spoil sports
In the late '70s, the MGB's glistening chrome front end would disappear, replaced by ugly rubber bumpers that made it look and handle like a dog.

with the 911 *(see pages 200–03),* but that was more of a GT machine, and even Ferrari only made token convertibles with a lift-off roof panel like the 308 GTS.

Then in the '90s the market changed once again. Carmakers had cynically exploited the performance sedan and stuck on one too many GT, GTi, S, and SE logos. Customers could see that most hot hatches were just souped-up versions of normal sedans. The market wanted niche cars, vehicles that said more about you than cash ever could, and it was the Japanese who reinvented the sports car first. When Mazda launched the MX-5 in 1990, it instantly kick-started a sports car revolution. Pretty, reliable, comfortable, and cheap, this was a roadster you didn't have to suffer to own. It may have been an unashamed copy of the '60s Lotus Elan *(see pages 176–79),* but its launch coincided with a consumer *crie de coeur* for something different. Sales went atomic and every single carmaker in the world started

Austin-Healey advertising

to look at sports cars in a completely different light.

Soon Rover had launched its MGF, Lotus its Elise, Porsche its Boxster, Mercedes its SLK, and Fiat its Barchetta. Audi fielded the TT, Jaguar chopped the roof off its XK8, Honda brought out the S2000, Ford reinvented the Thunderbird, and even prosaic old Vauxhall came up with the VX220. Suddenly the world wanted sports cars again, especially those mixing hi-tech engineering with retro looks. A booming world economy, disenchantment with bland sedans, and the desire to appear different fueled huge demand. Even long defunct brands like Jensen and AC cashed in and rolled out roadsters. And as I write that boom continues with

A bona fide sports car
Despite putting on a bit of weight during its life, Jaguar's E-Type epitomized the glorious era for British sports cars in the '50s and '60s.

The swinging six
The Triumph TR6 wasn't the last of the line, but it was the last of the respected TRs. And then came the '70s and the truly awful TR7.

Father of modern sportsters
Few personalities in the auto world have done as much to promote the sports ideal as the legendary Enzo Ferrari.

Jaguar looking at a modern E-Type replacement, Chrysler producing a budget two-seater, Lexus its SC430, plus a whole range of other sporty confections just waiting to be launched. The revolution in niche cars is now so strong that Ford has signed off its StreetKa concept for production – an ordinary supermini with a convertible top.

AN UNCERTAIN FUTURE

From being an expensive and impractical indulgence for the wealthy, the sports car has now become one of the most desirable and profitable products for the auto industry and one that looks set to be with us for some time to come. But for how long? When will this renaissance end? The answer to that lies in two factors that determine the longevity of the sports car market. One is large amounts of disposable income and the

other is political force. A worldwide recession could kill the sports car stone dead, but much more serious is the anti-car sentiments of governments. The two-seat sports car is the perfect embodiment of everything that's wrong with the car. It drinks too much fuel, goes too fast, and only accommodates two people. The indulgence of the sports car is what will finally end its reign forever. It really is an endangered species.

If you want to look at what sports cars of the future might look like, consider the Smart convertible. Frugal and space efficient, this open two-seater is still a niche product, but one with obvious environmental credentials. In other words, tomorrow's roadsters will be small, economical, and socially acceptable – and sadly a pale facsimile of their former selves. The selfish sports car hasn't got long. Maybe another decade at most. Its demise is inevitable. But when we attempt to write its epitaph we mustn't forget that of all the consumer durables created in the last century, the sports car is quite simply the most emotionally powerful of all. Its influence has been incredible and its effect far reaching. We may never be able to properly define the sports car, but we know that the world will be a much less interesting place without it.

Back to the future
Porsche has always been at
the cutting edge of trends
and technology, but
maintains a respect for its
sports car heritage. Its
redesigned 911 contains
echoes of the original
911 blueprint.

The Forties

"The granite-grey world of post-war austerity made the sports car as sexy as a platinum blonde."

THE EARLY SPORTS YEARS

1940

Through the Thirties the sports car was always a stern, uncompromising device. Weather protection was minimal, gearboxes hard to master, and ride quality washboard-hard. The sports car's close connection with motorsport made it less than user-friendly. Times, though, were changing and few customers actually wanted a car that could be realistically entered in serious competition; the pressure was on to create a more specialized, less unyielding machine.

And the most significant wind of change blew from Germany, where a svelte, silky confection with soft suspension, tubular chassis, and a small engine of amazing efficiency dramatically altered the whole course of the type's development. The 1936 BMW 328 (see pages 32–35) was a complete revelation, offering customers a poise, balance, and lightness of controls previously unheard of. But not only was the 328 astonishingly sweet to drive, it notched up a hugely convincing victory in the 1940 Mille Miglia, instantly setting the stage for a complete revaluation of sports car design.

POSTWAR INNOVATIONS

After the cessation of World War II, two British car companies effectively reinvented the sports car. One was MG and the other Jaguar. The MG TC of 1945

Timeline 1940s

Jaguar SS100

- British forces evacuated from Dunkirk.

- German forces enter Paris.

- The MG Car Company produces tanks and plane parts for the war effort.

- Bacon, butter, and sugar are rationed in Britain.

- Franklin Delano Roosevelt is re-elected as president of the US for a third term.

- The Japanese bomb Pearl Harbor; the US and Britain declare war on Japan the next day.

- The US starts work on the "Manhattan Project".

- The film How Green Was My Valley wins the best picture Academy Award.

- Hong Kong surrenders to the Japanese.

- US forces defeat the Japanese at Midway.

- The mass murder of millions of Jews in Nazi gas chambers begins.

- The first US jet airplane is tested by Bell Aircraft.

- The first automatic computer is developed in the United States.

- Magnetic tape recording is invented.

- Ellen Glasgow wins the Pulitzer Prize for her novel In This Our Life.

- The wartime "National Loaf" is introduced in Britain.

- 487 people die in a fire at the Coconut Grove nightclub in Boston.

- Allied forces land on island of Sicily.

- Surrender of Italy to Allied forces is announced by Eisenhower.

- Jackson Pollock holds his first one-man show.

- Charlie Chaplin marries Oona O'Neill.

- Penicillin is successfully used as a treatment for chronic diseases.

Cecil Kimber

- The first non-stop flight from London to Canada takes place.

- The D-Day landings in Normandy involve over 700 ships and 4,000 landing craft.

- Evelyn Waugh's book Brideshead Revisited is published.

Billboard advertising MG

| 1940 | 1941 | 1942 | 1943 | 1944 |

(see pages 24–27) may have looked prewar with its separate mudguards and spindly spoked wheels, but an enlarged cockpit, 1250cc engine, decent top, lights, and brakes made it disarmingly easy to drive. So much so that even American GIs, used to the labor-saving devices of transatlantic iron, bought TCs in droves. Car-starved Britain beat a path to the doors of the MG company not because the TC was a miracle of modern automotive packaging, but because it cost so little and drove so easily.

Jaguar, on the other hand, went several steps further, creating the first truly modern sports car, which was not only phenomenally cheap, but also sensationally fast and incredibly handsome. The XK120 of 1949 *(see pages 28–31)* had sweeping enclosed bodywork, a comfortable cabin, useable trunk, easy controls, and a glorious twin-cam engine that would run for years. Yes, the Moss gearbox was a bit crunchy, the drum brakes prone to fade, and the steering wheel still looked like it belonged on the bridge of a paddle steamer, but here was a sports car that wasn't just beautiful, but beautifully accessible too.

Instantly the sports car was no longer the preserve of the rich and physically fit but a hugely powerful consumer durable that magically conveyed youth on maturity and maturity on youth.

1945	1946	1947	1948	1949
• VE Day ends war in Europe. Japan surrenders on August 14. The war dead are estimated at 35 million.	• Juan Peron is elected president of Argentina.	• A US airplane is the first to fly at supersonic speeds.	• Jaguar Cars' XK Open Two Seater Super Sports is shown at the 1948 London Motor Show. The car is quickly renamed the XK120.	BMW 328 wins Le Mans
• The SS Car Company becomes Jaguar Cars Ltd.	• The xerography process is invented by Chester Carlson.	• The first Ferrari single-seater design is produced.	• The Porsche 356 is introduced.	• The new state of Israel is admitted to the United Nations. Israel's capital city is changed from Tel Aviv to Jerusalem.
• Production of the MG TC starts. Most are exported to the US.	• The US Navy tests an atomic bomb at Bikini atoll.	• British driver John Cobb establishes a world land speed record of 394.196 mph (634.655 km/h).	• The Olympic Games are held in London.	• Production of the MG TC ends after a run of 10,000 cars.
• BMW has a three-year production ban imposed on it because of its wartime activities.	• London airport opens for flights.	• Tennessee Williams is awarded the Pulitzer Prize for drama for *A Streetcar Named Desire*.		• The USSR tests its first atomic bomb, starting the Cold War in earnest.
	• The Nuremburg Tribunal ends, with 12 major Nazis sentenced to death. Hermann Goering commits suicide on the night before his scheduled execution.	• Princess Elizabeth marries Philip Mountbatten, Duke of Edinburgh.		
	• Albania, Hungary, Transjordan, and Bulgaria become independent states.	• Winter in Britain is the most severe since 1894.		
	• Britain and France evacuate Lebanon.	• "Flying saucers" are reported in the US.		

Jaguar XK120

Jaguar badge

JAGUAR
SS100

The SS100 was the world's first real sports car and the first truly sexy Jaguar. Visitors to the 1935 London Motor Show were left open-mouthed in amazement by its genuine 100 mph (161 km/h) performance, long hood, voluptuous fenders, and plush interior. And with light controls, close-fitting top, and strong sidescreens it was practical as well as gorgeous. But, best of all, at less than $2,500 (£500) it was a serious bargain, and one that could outperform virtually anything else on the road. To fully understand the SS100's impact you have to remember that back, in '35, for most people 100 mph (161 km/h) was unbelievably fast and 0 to 60 mph (96 km/h) in 10 seconds flat was like flying.

In 1937, a new 3-liter engine arrived and the SS100 proved to be a decent racer, with wins in the RAC Rallies of '37, '38, and '39. But with such fame and glamour came notoriety, and the slippery SS roadster soon became the chosen transportation of cads and bounders. Wiseguys with pencil-thin moustaches and slicked-back hair bought the car in droves, and even today some veteran car clubs are still rude about the SS100. Pedantry apart, it was the first really great Jag and the one that helped the tiny English car company establish a legendary reputation for slick two-seaters. Next to the E-Type Jag *(see pages 124–27)*, the SS100 is *the* ultimate sports car.

Top Cat
The star of the road was the choice of stars of the screen, though the 100's price of $2,000 (£395) made it affordable to many.

Making an impression
Word soon got out about the new racing Cat, and large crowds came to watch wherever it raced. The SS100 entered – and often won – events as diverse as international alpine trials and regional hill-climbs.

"With the SS100 Jaguar created one of the world's first great all-arounders, respected by serious car racing drivers and casual touring enthusiasts alike."

The successful SS – Jaguar's racing roots

The original 2½-liter-engined SS100 scored successes in rallies and sports car races, and the introduction of the 3½-liter engine in 1937 made the car a genuinely exciting racer when "stripped down" for extra speed. Driver Tommy Wisdom achieved a best lap of 118.02 mph (190.01 km/h) during a win in the 1937 Autumn Handicap in Brooklands, England. Other successes were notched up in the Villa Real sports car race – with Casimiro d'Oliveira at the wheel of a 2½-liter model – the Monte Carlo Rally, and the Alpine Rally, as well as a succession of RAC Rallies. The outbreak of war in 1939 brought an abrupt halt to racing and rallying. It also led to the abandonment of the SS company designation, as the initials became unshakeably associated with Hitler's black-uniformed terror elite. The company's postwar triumphs would come about under the more attractive name of Jaguar.

Front view

Rear view

Side view

Storage
Luggage could be stored behind the seats.

Top up
The top clipped onto the windshield frame.

Center-hinged hood
The engine could be easily accessed in vital race situations.

Wire wheel

Design and Production

Model	Jaguar SS100 (1935–41)
Production	N/A
Body style	Open two-seater sports.
Construction	Steel chassis with coachwork body.
Engines	2663.7cc and 3485cc straight-sixes.
Power output	125 bhp (3½-liter).
Transmission	Four-speed manual.
Suspension	Front and rear semi-elliptic leaf springs.
Brakes	Rod-operated drums all around.
Max speed	98 mph (158 km/h)

The man behind the success of the Jaguar SS100 was the young Bill Heynes, who joined SS Cars, Ltd. as William Lyons' first chief engineer in 1934, after being a draftsman with the Humber Company. He was aided by Harry Weslake, a consultant who had previously contributed to the development of Bentley engines. With an overhead valve replacing the side valve on the existing Standard engine, Heynes and Weslake turned a 70 bhp into a 100 bhp unit. The new 2½-liter engine was first installed in the immensely successful four-door Jaguar sedan. The company's first sports car, the SS90, introduced in the spring of 1935, still had the side-valve engine, but the new unit powered the SS100 when it was launched the following fall. A more powerful 3½-litre engine was introduced in 1937. The body of the car, however, remained unchanged until 1939, which brought a coupé model on the same chassis.

The precursor
(right) Before the SS100 came the 1935 SS90, an all-new racing model designed with the intention of giving SS Cars some high-profile exposure. Very similar in looks to the 100, just 23 examples of this fine sports car were built.

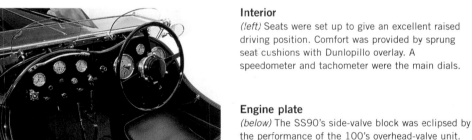

Lucas P100 headlight

Interior
(left) Seats were set up to give an excellent raised driving position. Comfort was provided by sprung seat cushions with Dunlopillo overlay. A speedometer and tachometer were the main dials.

Engine plate
(below) The SS90's side-valve block was eclipsed by the performance of the 100's overhead-valve unit.

High praise
(right) The 100 looked like a solid car and drove like one, too. A contemporary *Autocar* road test noted that, "it is a vivid car not easily to be equalled from point to point when suitably handled."

MG TC MIDGET

At the end of World War II, the automobile industry, along with the rest of the British economy, was faced with a period of reconstruction. One car that didn't need too much development, and was offered pretty much "off the shelf," was the MG TC Midget. This was because it was virtually the same as the MG TB that had come out in 1939. With no time to evolve the model during the war, MG decided to add slight modifications and rebadge it as the TC. Although essentially a prewar model, thereby inviting accusations that it was dated as soon as it was released, the TC was a surprising success. But maybe not that surprising; the twin-carb 1250cc engine was lively, handling was challenging yet rewarding, and, crucially, few other manufacturers were able to put out a "new" model so soon after the end of the war.

There was also the "GI factor" to consider – another reason put forward for the TC's success is that American military personnel stationed in Britain during the war fell in love with the sporty Midget and subsequently bought one when it was exported. Whether this is true or not, what's indisputable is that Detroit didn't make cars like this and a growing interest in sports cars helped the TC's US sales figures. MG's Midget would live on until the mid-Fifties, but the TC has pride of place for the sole reason that it opened up the American market for not just later Midgets, but also for hundreds of thousands of British sports cars.

Racing success
The TC was a popular sports model, especially in the US. This 1947 example is being raced by W.R. Chapman at the LMC Little Rally.

The basic TC – no-frills sports driving

Technically backward, the TC relied on the romantic sweep of its front wings to win its owners' hearts. There were no concessions to streamlining in its design, with exposed headlights and those separate wings arching over the narrow wire wheels. But if it was objectively not a very fast car, the TC still felt exciting with its rock-hard ride and tricky handling. It may not have provided much space inside, and was offered with absolutely no frills, but you could always add on an external luggage rack for touring. Although the TC is famous as the British car that cracked the American market, only one in five of those built actually crossed the Atlantic. American owners also had to accept an almost total lack of technical backup from MG. But then, half the fun of a TC was the tinkering needed to keep it on the road.

Front view

Rear view

Side view

"The TC began a successful export trend that really took off with the later TD."

Engine
The TC used the XPAG engine that was first placed into MG's TB in 1939 and would power all Midgets until a 1500cc version replaced it in 1955. One reason for the car's popularity was that the center-hinged hood allowed owners easy access to the engine.

Classic shape
The sweeping wings, separate headlights, and square front gave the TC an impressive overhead profile.

Design and Production

Model	MG TC Midget (1945–49)
Production	10,000
Body style	Two-door, two-seater sports.
Construction	Channel-section ladder-type chassis; ash-framed steel body.
Engine	Four-cylinder overhead valve 1250cc, with twin SU carburetors.
Power output	54 bhp at 5200 rpm.
Transmission	Four-speed with synchromesh on top three.
Suspension	Rigid front and rear axles on semi-elliptic springs, lever-type shock absorbers.
Brakes	Lockheed hydraulic drums.
Max speed	73 mph (117 km/h)

It was in the 1920s that Cecil Kimber, the manager of Lord Nuffield's Morris Garages (hence MG), came up with the idea of building cheap two-seaters using standard Morris parts. The T-series first appeared in 1935 with the TA Midget, followed in 1939 by the marginally-improved TB, and in 1945 by the even more marginally-updated TC. This shared with the prewar cars a wood-framed body, leaf-spring suspension, and 1250cc engine. Production methods at the MG Abingdon factory evolved as slowly as the cars, although, due to increased demand output in the late 1940s, was triple the 1930s level. The MG TD replaced the TC in 1949. Mixing elements of the MG TC and the YA-type MG sedan, it was not exactly revolutionary. The TD used the same 1250cc engine, although coil-spring suspension gave a smoother ride. The TF, the last of the T-series introduced in 1953, made moves toward streamlining with headlights set into the wings, and, eventually, brought an upgrade to a 1466cc engine. Almost 50,000 postwar T-series cars were built – 10,000 of them were TCs.

The MG guru
(left) The originator of the MG brand in 1922, Cecil Kimber was obsessed with performance. His tuned Morris Oxford won the London to Land's End Trial in 1923 and set MG on the road to greatness. He died in 1945, the same year as the release of the TC.

Limited space
There was not much room for either the passengers or their luggage.

Interior
(right) Large Jaeger dials were set into a stylish curved dashboard and included a tachometer on the right and a speedometer directly in front of the passenger on the left.

Road and track
(left) Silverstone was the setting for this TC's race, but the model was raced more abroad. Its modest power output and limited top speed provided a gentle introduction to the world of racing and helped kick-start the careers of many drivers, including one world champion, Phil Hill.

JAGUAR XK120

The foundations of Jaguar's beautiful XK120 were laid down during World War II. With car production put on hold, the company spent time developing a new engine, which it planned to fit into an as yet undesigned sedan model. By the time the 1948 Earl's Court Motor Show came around in London, the XK unit had been placed into a "prototype" called the Jaguar Super Sports. The idea behind it was to stimulate postwar interest in Jaguar by producing a short production run, prestige showstopper. And boy did it work. Visitors to the show were bowled over by the Super Sports' gorgeous design, incorporating a refreshing purity of line. Not only that, it was also sensationally fast; the XK120 production model that went on sale from 1949 proved that 120 really did stand for 120 mph (193 km/h), making it the fastest production car in the world.

But Jaguar was caught somewhat off guard by the overwhelming reaction to the car. The original Super Sports had been hand-built in aluminum, and tooling now had to be set up for a less costly, metal-bodied production model. It meant that aside from the lucky 240 or so able to secure further hand-built examples in 1949, eager buyers had to wait until 1950 when production lines were fully operational. And it was well worth the wait. Offered in a choice of roadster, convertible, or coupé, the XK120 was a genuine thing of beauty and, crucially for Jaguar, a phenomenal success in the US.

Star cachet
You needed a name like Clark Gable to get your hands on one of the first few XK120s to come off the production line in 1949.

Star billing
One of the first instances of a Jaguar making an appearance in a movie was this XK120 in the 1957 production, *Island in the Sun*.

Versatile racer
As well as track wins, the XK120 got a number of rally laurels. Here, NUB 120, driven by Ian Appleyard, competes in the 1950 International Alpine Rally, where it won an Alpine Cup that year as well as in '52 and '53.

The dynamic Cat – a contemporary classic

The XK120 established its claim to be the world's fastest production car with an early demonstration run that hit 132.596 mph (213.47 km/h) – although the production version's accepted maximum speed was 120 mph (193 km/h). In 1950, XK120s took the top three places in the Dunrod TT, but less happily failed to make much impact at Le Mans. By the following year, Jaguar had developed a racing version of the XK120, the C-Type, which plentifully compensated for this failure. The original XK120 roadster was joined by a coupe in 1951 and a convertible in 1953. The only drawbacks of these impressive cars were that the steering and braking were not fully adequate for the performance. In the course of the 1950s, the introduction of disc brakes and rack-and-pinion steering improved both stopping and handling as the power of the engine increased.

Front view

Rear view

Side view

"The coupes are often regarded as the most gorgeous of the XK120s."

Design and Production

Model	Jaguar XK120 (1949–54)
Production	12,055
Body styles	Two-seater roadster, coupe, and convertible.
Construction	Separate chassis, aluminum/steel body.
Engine	3442cc twin overhead cam six-cylinder, twin SU carburetors.
Power output	160 bhp at 5100 rpm.
Transmission	Four-speed manual, Moss transmission with synchromesh on upper three ratios.
Suspension	Front: independent, wishbones and torsion bars; Rear: live rear axle, semi-elliptic.
Brakes	Hydraulically-operated 12-in (30-cm) drums.
Max speed	126 mph (203 km/h)

The sweeping lines of the body that William Lyons designed for the XK120 made it an irrepressibly desirable object to own. Continuing the prewar Jaguar tradition of providing style and performance at a reasonable price, the original hand-built aluminum model sold for $4,000 (£998), under half the cost of any comparable car then on the market. The XK unit was the first engine designed and produced entirely by Jaguar. Previously, the Standard Company had supplied the powerplants, but this relationship had become increasingly unsatisfactory. The XK was created by a team set up by Bill Heynes, with engineers Claude Baily and Walter Hassan as key figures. The classic engine they produced went on to power tanks as well as Le Mans winners. Through the XK120's successors – the XK140 of 1954 and the 1957 XK150 – the XK series stayed in production until the end of the 1950s.

The boss
(*left*) Sir William Lyons went from Swallow sidecars to creating one of the most famous car brands in the world. His ability to produce a succession of high-performance cars at affordable prices was unmatched.

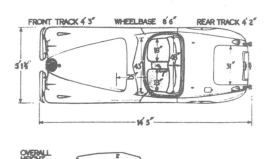

Dimensions
(*above*) As with all other Jaguars, much time was spent making sure the XK120 was beautifully proportioned.

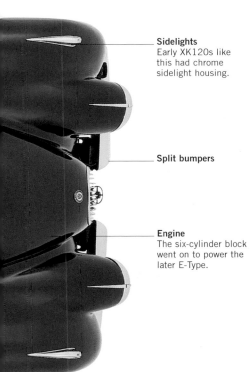

Sidelights
Early XK120s like this had chrome sidelight housing.

Split bumpers

Engine
The six-cylinder block went on to power the later E-Type.

Sporting successor
(*above*) The XK120 provided the basis for the C-Type (*see pages 48–51*), which continued Jaguar's winning sequence of race successes.

Soft focus
(*left*) These images taken from an original sales brochure show the very first XK120 built, with added airbrushing. Not that this beautiful car needed tricks to improve its looks!

Foreign success
International long-distance rallies
proved well within the capabilities
of the all-conquering 328.

Individual wind protection
The 328's novel split windshield could be folded
down separately on the driver's or passenger's
side, or completely in one piece.

All-terrain racer
Cross-country racing was sometimes taken to the extreme, but the 328's well-constructed chassis could handle even the bumpiest of riverbeds.

Supreme machine
The presence of a 328 on an race entry list put fear into its competitors, and it was unfortunate that World War II put an end to its legendary series of victories.

BMW 328

Let's not mince words. The 328 is one of the most important sports cars ever. Launched in 1936, it created the same fuss as the Jaguar E-Type did in 1961 *(see pages 124–27)*. Even today a well-driven 328 can tickle the tailfeathers of contemporary BMWs and annihilate most hot hatchbacks. Exotic, fast, handsome, and technically ingenious, 328s ruled prewar race circuits, and their finest hour was coming in first, third, fifth, and sixth in the 1940 Mille Miglia. Legend has it that a 3½-liter special was tested on an autobahn in 1940 and reached an astonishing 157 mph (253 km/h). With a tubular chassis, independent front suspension, rack-and-pinion steering, hydraulic brakes, and hemispherical combustion chambers, the 328 was so ahead of its time it made other sports cars drive like donkey carts.

Dramatically modern-looking, those sweeping fenders, tunneled headlights, and canted radiator grille are claimed to have inspired the shape of Jaguar's XK120 *(see pages 28–31),* and Sir William Lyons was known to have been mightily impressed by the 328's performance and handling. After the war, one of the Mille Miglia cars was brought to Britain as part of reparations payments, and in 1946 appeared wearing a new grille as a Frazer Nash. Bristol Cars also based their new models on 328 technology, and that sweet-spinning 2-liter engine was used in ACs and racing Cooper Bristols. The BMW 328 is exhilarating, beautiful, powerful, and controllable; the perfect definition of what makes a sports car truly great.

The racing BMW – setting high standards

The BMW 328 was designed for competition and won prestigious victories in the hands of famous drivers of the 1930s such as Prince Bira, Ernest Henna, and Dick Seaman. At the last Le Mans race before the war in 1939, 328s took fifth, seventh, and ninth places. The specially-streamlined model that won the Brescia Mille Miglia in 1940 averaged 103.6 mph (166.8 km/h). But the car was equally at home in the more modest context of hill-climbs and sprints. The 328 set the modern style for all-enveloping bodywork, with the splashguards attached firmly to the main body structure and completely covering the wheels and suspension. The styling has proved to have enduring appeal – it was paid the compliment of exact if superficial imitation in the 1970s with the Sbarro Replica, which repeats every detail of the 328's appearance in fiberglass.

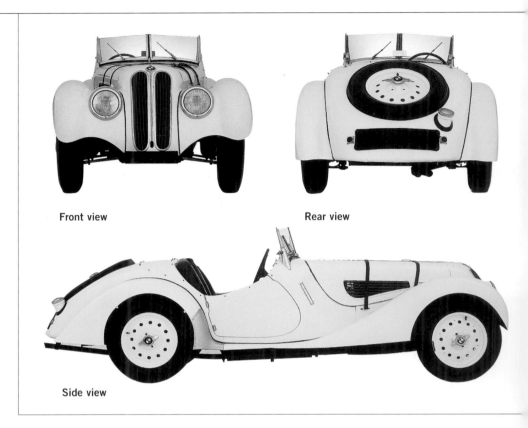

Front view

Rear view

Side view

"The 328 totally dominated contemporary racing."

Hood strap

New-wave design
Splashguards
integral to the
body were rare
at the time.

Rear-hinged door

Design and Production

Model	BMW 328 (1936–40)
Production	462 plus five special racers.
Body style	Two-seater convertible.
Construction	Twin tube chassis with box-section cross members. Alloy body.
Engine	1971cc straight-six.
Power output	80–150 bhp.
Transmission	Four-speed manual.
Suspension	Front: independent lower wishbones with transverse leaf spring; Rear: semi-elliptic springs.
Brakes	Drums all around.
Max speed	110 mph (177 km/h)

The German car industry in the 1930s enjoyed every support from the Nazi regime. Adolf Hitler, an automobile enthusiast, declared car manufacturing the key industry of the future. The world-class BMW 328 was the perfect car to sweep along Germany's newly-built autobahns, in its style, handling, and performance. The 328 certainly was a masterpiece of innovative technology, from its welded steel tubular frame to its exceptional straight-six engine, devised by engineering genius Fritz Feidler. The inclined valves in its hemispherical combustion chambers were operated by an ingenious "crossover" mechanism. Conventional pushrods activated the inlet valves, while additional horizontal pushrods crossed over them to operate the exhaust valves. This boosted output from 55 to 80 bhp. It is ironic that Feidler's engine ended up powering British sports cars after the war.

Streamlined rear
The spare wheel was "sunk" into the rear of the car.

Holding it together
(right) The tubular chassis frame was almost the same as that on previous BMWs, with the members cut from sheet steel and then rolled into tubes. Combined with great suspension and that wonderful six-cylinder powerplant, it provided the 328 with unparalleled roadholding.

Adoring crowds
(left) The 328 attracted attention wherever it raced. Unlike other racers, it always competed with a full spec of headlights and splashguards.

National pride
(left) Period advertising declared the 328 to be Germany's premier sports car. And most would have agreed that the production model's ability to hit 100 mph (161 km/h) with such ease, combined with the competition version's 120 bhp output, probably made the 328 the most complete sports model in the world.

Der erfolgreiche deutsche Sportwagen

The Fifties

"The personality and allure of the modern sports car flowered in the Fifties."

THE CLASSIC YEARS

1950

The Fifties was the sports car's most fertile decade. The two-seat roadster had become a suburban trinket, a toy even, and almost completely divorced from the brutal, rough-riding competition machine of 20 years earlier. A new set of parameters dictated that sports cars didn't only have to be convertibles, they could be hardtops too. A modern-looking aerodynamic body was a must, along with accommodation for two in real comfort (and even space for two little ones in relative discomfort). Room for a suitcase or two was also essential, plus niceties like heaters, wind-down windows, and map-reading lights. Performance-wise, 100 mph (161 km/h) became the speed benchmark, and anything much faster was considered frighteningly modern.

RISING STANDARDS

Although the Porsche 356 of 1950 (see pages 108–11) could only manage 85 mph (137 km/h), its wind-evading shape, spacious cabin, and rewarding road responses established it as a breed apart. The svelte MGA of 1955 (see pages 76–79) may have looked more rakish, but the little Porsche brought a new imperative to the sports car genre: engineering excellence. The two-seater could now be technically audacious, rewarding its lucky

Timeline 1950s

• Alfa Romeo unveils the 1900 – a family sedan that is also a sports car.	• In the Korean War, UN forces take "Heartbreak Ridge," north of Yanguu.	**Alfa Romeo logo** • The first contraceptive pills are produced.	• The prototype Chevrolet Corvette "Dream Car" is shown at the General Motors Motorama in New York City.	**Ford Thunderbird** • Ford begins production of the Thunderbird sports car.
• The estimated population of the world is 2.3 billion.	• Morgan wins the team award in Britain's RAC rally with its Plus Four model.	• Anti-British riots take place in Egypt.	• The Alfa Romeo Spider is introduced.	• The Morgan Four Four is reintroduced as the Series 2.
• US legislation is passed that severely restricts Communists and forbids members of totalitarian groups to enter the US.	• Aston Martin launches the DB3.	• Britain's first atomic tests are carried out in the Monte Bello Islands in Western Australia.	• Stalin dies in the USSR and is succeeded by Malenkov. Kruschev becomes first secretary of the Communist Party.	• The Porsche 356 Speedster is launched.
• Two Puerto Ricans attempt to assassinate US President Truman.	• Color television is first introduced in the US.	• SS United States wins the Blue Riband, after crossing the Atlantic in only 3 days, 10 hours.		• Roger Bannister runs a mile in 3 minutes and 59.4 seconds.
Jaguar C-Type		• Mass escapes from East to West Berlin begin.		
		• King George VI dies and is succeeded by his daughter, Queen Elizabeth II.		
		• Agatha Christie's The Mousetrap opens in London.		
1950	**1951**	**1952**	**1953**	**1954**

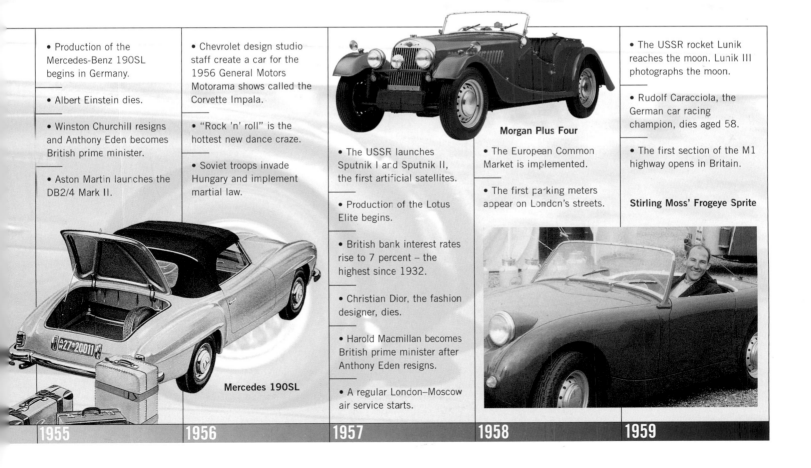

owner with the tactile bounty of controls that talked to you. The average driver could now tear through corners, play tunes on his gearbox, and practice fishtails safely. The sports car had become fun.

Then in 1954 the new sports car rulebook was torn to shreds. The incredibly avant-garde Mercedes 300SL was a vision of the future. The first true postwar supercar, it could hit 150 mph (242 km/h), had a multitubular space frame body, peerless aerodynamic credentials, fuel injection, and, if you bought the coupe rather than the roadster, those glorious gullwing doors. Nobody cared that it cost more than two Jaguar XK140s – the 300SL was so modern it made you want to burst out cheering.

But those who couldn't afford the stratospheric price tag of the Mercedes were still happy to scorch around in a cornucopia of '50s rockets. Cars like the AC Ace, Jag XKs, Lotus Elite, Alfa Spiders, and Triumph TRs offered daring looks and creditable performance yet didn't cost the world. Most were reasonably reliable, simple to drive, and easy to own. The sports car was maturing nicely and generating plenty of profit for its makers. MG made a million dollars from its MGA, and every European auto mogul was desperate to carve a niche in what was becoming the most lucrative market, the US, where 80 percent of all sports cars were sold.

1955
- Production of the Mercedes-Benz 190SL begins in Germany.
- Albert Einstein dies.
- Winston Churchill resigns and Anthony Eden becomes British prime minister.
- Aston Martin launches the DB2/4 Mark II.

1956
- Chevrolet design studio staff create a car for the 1956 General Motors Motorama shows called the Corvette Impala.
- "Rock 'n' roll" is the hottest new dance craze.
- Soviet troops invade Hungary and implement martial law.

1957
- The USSR launches Sputnik I and Sputnik II, the first artificial satellites.
- Production of the Lotus Elite begins.
- British bank interest rates rise to 7 percent – the highest since 1932.
- Christian Dior, the fashion designer, dies.
- Harold Macmillan becomes British prime minister after Anthony Eden resigns.
- A regular London–Moscow air service starts.

Morgan Plus Four

1958
- The European Common Market is implemented.
- The first parking meters appear on London's streets.

1959
- The USSR rocket Lunik reaches the moon. Lunik III photographs the moon.
- Rudolf Caracciola, the German car racing champion, dies aged 58.
- The first section of the M1 highway opens in Britain.

Stirling Moss' Frogeye Sprite

Mercedes 190SL

Earlier model
The DB3 came before the DB3S, but was slow, underdeveloped, and not very competitive.

Quality bloodline
(right) Aston Martin has consistently produced thoroughbred British sports cars, commanding respect across the driving world.

Aston Martin DB1

Aston Martin DB3S FHC

ASTON MARTIN
DB3S

The DB3S was a smaller, lighter version of David Brown's first real racer, the DB3. A particularly fine example of reductive engineering with its gaping gothic wheelarches and narrower chassis tubes, Willie Watson's DB3S of 1953 was one of Aston's most important postwar competition cars. After a disastrous debut at Le Mans, where all three cars dropped out, the new Aston won its remaining five races that year, including the Goodwood 9-hours and the Tourist Trophy – the team's first victory in a world championship event. But instead of developing an already very competitive machine, Aston was forced to pursue David Brown's dream of the disastrous V12 Lagonda.

Ironically, it was scores of independent racers who forced Aston to build a limited production run of 20 further cars, at an astonishingly expensive $10,900 (£3,901). Throughout the '50s Britain watched some spectacular battles between the dark-green Astons and Jag C-Types *(see pages 48–51)*, and the curvaceous Aston really put the little company on the map. By the time it was superseded by the DBR in 1956, the DB3S was pushing out 230 bhp and had become a British motorsport icon.

Aston Martin DB2/4   Aston Martin DB4 DHC   Aston Martin DB MkIII

Aston's superlative DB3S – pure automotive art

In 1947 wealthy industrialist David Brown took over Aston Martin and Lagonda so that he could give free rein to his passion for sports cars. To begin the series of cars that were to bear his initials, he brought together a prototype under development by Aston Martin with a 2.6-liter twin-cam six-cylinder engine designed by Lagonda technical director W.O. Bentley. The DB2, which started its career in 1950, was both a sports and sales success. The DB3S appeared in 1952. The aim of this car was to win races. Although recognized as a production model by the sports authorities, it was not in any sense a true road car – there was no top or passenger door. The DB3S scored a number of sports successes in 1953–54, but on the whole was more admired for the style of its curvaceous light alloy body than for pure performance.

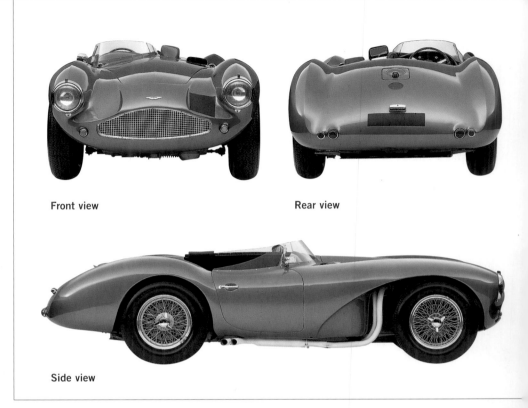

Front view

Rear view

Side view

Engine
Early engines were exactly as used in the DB3, developing 182 bhp at 5500 rpm, but final drive was changed to a lighter alloy cased spiral bevel drive. The cooling system remained largely unchanged too, apart from the repositioning of the header tank.

Later revisions
A few of the last team racing DB3Ss had a revised front section with faired-in headlights.

"The exquisite lines of the DB3S make it one of *the* ultimate sports cars."

Aero screen
Low-profile racing windshield.

Design and Production

Model	Aston Martin DB3S (1953–56)
Production	20 production road cars plus 11 factory racers.
Body styles	Two-seat sports racer plus five closed coupes.
Construction	Alloy body with tubular chassis.
Engines	2922cc straight-six.
Power output	182–240 bhp.
Transmission	Four-speed manual.
Suspension	Front: independent with trailing links and torsion bars; Rear: De Dion axle, trailing links and transverse torsion bars.
Brakes	Drums all around (Girling discs used in 1954).
Max speed	130 mph (209 km/h)

The chassis and suspension for the DB3 were designed by Eberan von Eberhorst, who was already famous through his association with Auto-Union and Cisitalia. The DB3S that followed differed from the DB3 in being lighter and having a shorter wheelbase. The 2922cc powerplant was a direct descendant of the Lagonda engine used in the DB2, but it delivered 180 bhp as standard compared with 125 bhp for the DB2 unit, and it could be souped-up to deliver 210 bhp. The car had a tubular frame ladder chassis with trailing link independent front suspension and a De Dion rear suspension. There was rack-and-pinion steering and a four-speed manual gearbox. Drum brakes were standard on production cars, although the disc brakes used for factory racing models were sometimes used on production cars by request. The car was put into production – at least after a fashion – at the Aston Martin factory at Feltham, England, in 1953, although only 31 were ever built, and that included factory racing cars. Brown was so indifferent to the profit potential of his hobby that he marketed the production versions of the DB3S at below cost price.

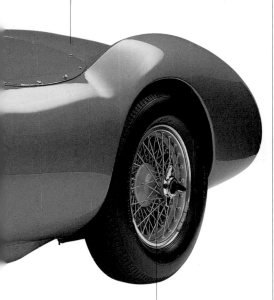

Race adjustment
Metal panel used to enclose unused passenger seat on racers.

Braking system
The DB3S had drum brakes, but front discs were used on later models.

Aston schooling
(left) Many '50s racing legends learned their craft twirling the wheel of a DB3S, including Stirling Moss, Caroll Shelby, Roy Salvadori, Reg Parnell, and Tony Brooks. All remember the car fondly and praised its disarming poise, urge, and balance.

Interior
(right) The stark and functional cockpit was typical of '50s racers. Production DB3S road cars were two-seaters and could carry a willing passenger, while racing versions blanked off the second seat with a flush metal panel. Secondary tachometer and fire extinguisher are later modern fixtures.

Base model
(left) The DB3 was the forerunner to the DB3S and was inadequate in many ways. A crude chassis, not enough power, excess weight, and reliability problems precluded any serious competition success.

JAGUAR XKSS

We may never know the real reasons for the creation of the Jaguar XKSS. Some say that Sir William Lyons, faced with 26 unwanted D-Types, told his engineers to turn them into road cars. Others claim that that the XKSS was an attempt to make the D-Type eligible for American racing by producing a street-legal version. Factory driver Duncan Hamilton insisted that he inspired the car by modifying his D-Type for road use. Whatever, the race-spec D-Types were equipped with bumpers, windshields, and headlight cowls.

The first car was sent to New York on a sales tour that generated 50 orders. But in February 1957, a fire destroyed several unfinished cars. Getting the factory running again was the priority, and the XKSS was canned. The fire had been reported worldwide and Jaguar was besieged with orders. And with such mystique surrounding the XKSS, it's no wonder that the 16 surviving cars now have a price tag measured in millions.

Racing heart
As the XKSS was basically a D-Type for the road, it had no problem tackling circuits such as this one in Brooklands, England. A few of the remaining XKSSs are still exhibited at tracks today.

Imposing presence
The XKSS had a futuristic profile,
especially when compared with the
average models on the roads in the
late '50s. But this rarity was the
nucleus of a Jaguar model that would
soon be seen in far greater numbers
on streets all over the world – the
E-Type *(see pages 124–27).*

The sublime XKSS – a landmark rarity

The XKSS' origins lay in the D-Type, introduced in 1954 as the racing successor to Jaguar's C-Type *(see pages 48–51)*. The sensational curvaceous shape was the product of wind-tunnel research and advanced mathematics, a scientific design operation led by Malcolm Sayer. Powered by the twin-cam XK engine, the D-Type dominated the Le Mans 24-hour race in the mid-1950s. Narrowly failing to win on its debut in 1954, it went on to triumph for three years in succession from 1955. Whatever motive led Sir William Lyons (the knighthood came in 1956) to turn the D into the street-legal XKSS, the product was supremely exciting and potentially practical – if you wanted you could drive it around town. The idea behind the XKSS would come to fruition four years later in the E-Type *(see pages 124–27)*.

Front view

Rear view

Side view

Full length
The whole of the hood hinged forward, a boon for engine tinkerers.

Squeezing in
Small hinge-down doors enhanced the impression of entering a cockpit.

"The XKSS was an outstanding blend of race performance and a design based on precision aerodynamics."

Design and Production

Model	Jaguar XKSS (1957)
Production	16
Body style	Two-seat sports racer.
Construction	Semi-monocoque alloy and steel frame.
Engine	3442cc straight-six.
Power output	250 bhp.
Transmission	Four-speed manual.
Suspension	Front: unequal length wishbones with torsion bar; Rear: trailing links and torsion bars.
Brakes	Dunlop discs front and rear.
Max speed	144 mph (232 km/h)

The XKSS body had a magnesium alloy monocoque center section and tail bolted to a multitubular steel front frame that supported the engine, transmission, and suspension. The hood and front fenders were another discrete unit. The engine was the XK six-cylinder twin-overhead-camshaft 3442cc unit, delivering 250 bhp. Some factory D-Types had fuel-injection, but this was never used in production models or XKSSs. To turn the D-Type into

the XKSS, Jaguar added a passenger door, a full-width windshield, and a folding top, while removing the driver's headrest and the central divide between driver and passenger. Practically ineffectual, but neat, thin bumpers were added at the four corners. The fire at the Jaguar factory in February 1957 ended production of the XKSS for good. Of the 16 XKSSs produced before the fire, 14 were sold in the US, one went to Hong Kong, and one remained in the UK.

Engine
(right) The glorious six-pot, twin-cam XK unit is an automotive legend. Triple Weber carbs gave huge urge and unburstable longevity. Simple chain-driven cam layout with two valves per cylinder proved enormously reliable and temperament-free. The optional high axle ratio gave a genuine 160 mph (258 km/h).

Body panels
Hand-beaten aluminum panels were a nightmare to align and no two were ever the same.

Interior
(left) Inside was simple, with Smiths white-on-black gauges and wood-rim wheel. Warning lights and switches were shared with contemporary Jaguar sedans. The 180 mph (290 km/h) speedometer was unprecedented in the '50s.

Novel rear entry
The trunk was reached via a neat fold-down rear flap on the SS's curvaceous rump.

Making the D
(above) A period shot of Browns Lane production lines shows the XKSS's forebear, the D-Type, gradually being rolled toward final assembly and the paint shop. The telltale rear fin was always a D-Type trademark.

JAGUAR
C-TYPE

The story of the C-Type is the stuff of sporting legend. The extraordinary success of Jaguar's XK120 *(see pages 28–31)* persuaded company boss Bill Lyons to develop a racing model to compete with the all-conquering Ferraris at Le Mans, and he set about the task with characteristic zeal. With the fast, reliable XK powerplant having already established itself as a potential race-winner, modified XK120s were put through their paces in 1950, and a year later, an XK120C (C-Type) prototype made a winning debut at Le Mans. Though restyled 1952 models failed to gain honors that year – overheating meant all three cars were forced to retire – C-Types gained first and second places in '53 in a record average speed of over 105 mph (169 km/h). By this time, Jaguar had well and truly earned a place at the top table of Europe's racing elite.

The structurally similar D-Type replaced the C in 1954 and continued Jaguar's amazing sequence of big-race victories by winning the 24-hour race for three consecutive years from 1955 to '57. In the meantime, those private racers who had bought C-Types were enjoying them for use on the road as well as the track – many would actually drive them to and from races. After their days as competitive racers were over, they were often used as high-performance highway tourers. Just 53 examples were produced, which makes this seminal Cat one of the most sought after collectors' cars around.

Worldwide racer
The C-Type had been designed with the prestigious Le Mans 24-hour race in mind, but it also competed in smaller events. The Isle of Man was the setting for this 1953 International British Empire Trophy race.

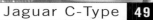

European circuit
Stirling Moss waits to go off in his
C-Type at the 1953 Mille Miglia.

First-time win
Moss drove one of the three C-Types at Le Mans in
'51, though the Walker and Whitehead duo won.

Sterling driver
The young Stirling Moss became synonymous with the
Jaguar brand, making his name in XK120s and C-Types.

The race-honed C-Type – a Le Mans legend

The C-Type was designed to win races at the top level of motorsport, and that essentially meant the Le Mans 24-hour race. Peter Walker and Peter Whitehead duly drove a prototype C-Type to victory at Le Mans first time out in 1951 with a record-breaking average speed of 93.5 mph (150.5 km/h). The following year brought severe disappointment for Jaguar at Le Mans when hastily implemented changes to the design led to overheating, forcing all their entries to retire. But in 1953, the C-Types returned in style, now equipped with disc brakes and with triple Weber carburetors to give the engine extra power. The Jaguars took first place with Tony Rolt and Duncan Hamilton, and second with Peter Walker and Stirling Moss, the winning car averaging 105.85 mph (170.5 km/h), the first time the race speed had topped the hundred mark.

Front view

Rear view

Side view

"The C-Type was designed purely with winning in mind, a task it accomplished in emphatic style."

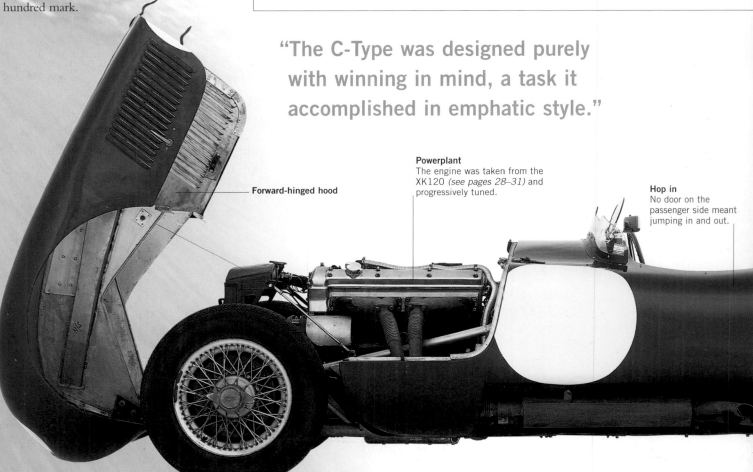

Forward-hinged hood

Powerplant
The engine was taken from the XK120 (see pages 28–31) and progressively tuned.

Hop in
No door on the passenger side meant jumping in and out.

Design and Production

Model	Jaguar C-Type (1951–53)
Production	53
Body style	Two-door, two-seater sports racer.
Construction	Tubular chassis, aluminum body.
Engine	Jaguar XK120 3442cc, six-cylinder, double overhead camshaft with twin SU carburetors.
Power output	200–210 bhp at 5800 rpm.
Transmission	Four-speed XK transmission with close-ratio gears.
Suspension	Torsion bars all around; wishbones at front, rigid axle at rear.
Brakes	Lockheed hydraulic drums; later cars used Dunlop discs all around.
Max speed	144 mph (232 km/h)

Asked to produce a racing version of the XK120, the Jaguar design team shed weight from the original by creating a space-frame chassis and making the body of aluminum, rather than the steel of the XK120. Rack-and-pinion steering and a redesigned suspension improved handling at high speed. The shape was refined by designer Malcolm Sayer for maximum aerodynamic efficiency and the XK engine upgraded for extra power. Initially equipped with conventional drum brakes, C-Types were later equipped with discs, a notable innovation imported from the aircraft industry. Regular production of C-Types at Jaguar's Coventry, England, factory began in August, 1952 and continued for about a year. Many of the total of 53 built were shipped to the US, where there were more buyers for what was an understandably expensive car – selling in Britain for $6,500 (£2,300).

Tunnel tests
(right) Malcom Sayer's aerodynamic design was put to the test in a wind tunnel. His aircraft industry experience shone through as the C-Type's resistance figures were impressive.

Le Mans winner
(left) Duncan Hamilton and Tony Rolt set the racing world on fire when they drove this C-Type to victory at the 1953 Le Mans 24-hour race.

Interior
The cockpit was purely functional, with just a couple of dials on the dash. A grab handle was provided for the passenger.

Beauty and function
(above) The C-Type was made up of the XK120 unit put into a special frame and cloaked with a streamlined aluminum body.

Early days
(left) One of the original C-Types is assembled at the Jaguar factory. The hinged hood allowed easy engine access when making mid-race adjustments; the early model often overheated.

MORGAN
PLUS FOUR

It's hard to imagine that such a traditional-looking car is still being produced today. Even more surprising is that the first four-wheeled Morgans from which the Plus Four was derived came out way back in 1936. Previously, Henry Morgan had successfully produced trikes, but then transferred to four-wheelers and, after developing a series of two- and four-door models, the Plus Four was released in 1951. Incorporating a 2088cc Vanguard engine, it immediately achieved racing honors by getting the team award in both the 1951 and '52 RAC Rallies in England.

By the time the last Plus Four was rolled out in 1969, the model had been through a succession of engine upgrades – based on the TR units – as well as a few minor styling modifications. Aside from that, the Plus Four looked essentially the same as the original, and very similar to the current Morgan line-up.

Morgan pioneers
(below) In 1939, a Morgan finished in a very respectable 15th position at Le Mans.

Top of the class
(below right) This Morgan secured a class win at the 1956 M.C.C. National Rally.

"Morgan is a rare example of a company persisting
with a conventional design and remaining strong
in the face of gizmo-laden modern competitors."

Touring capability
Pneumatic cushions for the
driver and passenger
combined with a patented
Morgan suspension system
ensured fair levels of
comfort on longer trips.

Consistently Morgan – traditional and proud

What is most striking about the Morgan Plus Four is what there is not to be said about it – no radical changes in styling, no dramatic innovations in engineering or materials, just the same excellent car produced through two decades. And these were decades of especially rapid change in society, as well as in sports cars. Under the hood there was a steady increase in power, culminating with the TR4 engine in the 1960s, which merited the introduction of front-wheel disc brakes. But the most that happened to the look of the Plus Four was the shift to a mildly-angled radiator and semi-recessed headlights in the mid-1950s. It is amusing and instructive that Morgan's only attempt to go modern, with the Plus-Four-Plus fiberglass-bodied coupé in 1964, went down like a lead balloon with the company's traditonal clientele. Only 50 were ever built.

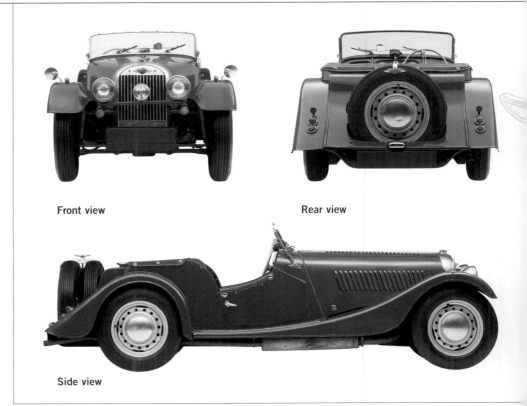

Front view

Rear view

Side view

Engine
The original 2088cc Vanguard unit put out 68 bhp, but by the time the Plus Four Plus was introduced in 1963, Morgan had equipped the car with a 2138cc Triumph TR4 block capable of 105 bhp.

Door styles
Some models had rear-hinged "suicide" doors, though this example has the front-hinged variety.

Traditional hood latch

Design and Production

Model	Morgan Plus Four (1951–69)
Production	3,737
Body styles	Two- and four-seater sports convertible.
Construction	Steel chassis, ash frame, steel and alloy outer panels.
Engines	2088cc overhead-valve inline four (Vanguard); 1991cc or 2138cc overhead-valve in-line four (TR).
Power output	105 bhp at 4700 rpm (2138cc TR engine).
Transmission	Four-speed manual.
Suspension	Front: sliding stub axles, coil springs, and telescopic shocks; Rear: live axle, semi-elliptic leaf springs, and lever-arm shocks.
Brakes	Drums front and rear; front discs standard from 1960.
Max speed	100 mph (161 km/h)

When the Plus Four first appeared in 1951, the Morgan company advertised it as "a comfortable long-distance touring car and one that will give a long life of economical and trouble-free motoring." This was a company that understood the values of its conservative clientele. Morgan was almost apologetic that "the modern tendency" to demand "a higher performance (particularly in our Overseas Markets)" had led to the adoption of a larger powerplant, the Standard Vanguard engine. Presumably Morgan's British customers had no objection to a bit of power, however, because the even livelier TR2 unit was introduced from 1955. In keeping with the traditional style and feel of Morgan cars, production methods at the company's Malvern works remained in a 1930s' timewarp. Morgan was not only family owned, but often employed families from father to son.

Body shop
(left) Because Morgan has retained most of the production methods of its predecessors, this scene would not be too different to that in the current body shop. Keeping output low has always guaranteed a waiting list to buy Morgan cars and at the same time kept prices high.

Proud body
(right) The Morgan's brochure stated that "the body work on all models is coach built with the best materials, of distinctive design, simple, light, and easily repaired." Thousands of buyers who bought the two- or four-seater Sports Coupe and Convertible attested to this.

Top cover compartment

Twin spare tires

Winning ads
(left) Magazine advertisements listed Morgan's race successes in a number of rallies. What was even more impressive was that these victories came very soon after the company put out its first four-wheeled models; the company's "Pin Your Faith on the Morgan 4-4" motto really did have some substance.

TRIUMPH TR2

There's no doubt that the TR2 embodied the spirit of the British sports car "tradition" in the Fifties. What is surprising, though, is that this was Triumph's first attempt at producing a sports model. The TR2 was first seen under the guise of the Triumph Sports prototype at the 1952 Earl's Court Show in London, where it was somewhat overshadowed by crowds flocking to see the new Austin-Healey. A year later, however, a revamped TR2 received the praise it deserved when it exhibited at the Geneva Motor Show.

The TR2's origins were partially down to the fortunes of one of its competitors. Following the American success of Jaguar's XK120 *(see pages 28–31)*, which had been triumphantly unleashed three years previously, Triumph saw its own chance to break into this lucrative market. With the aim of producing an inexpensive two-seater sports car, the company created a prototype, though it was a bit of a stylistic mess and its handling was pretty poor. By the time the car reached Geneva, it had a new chassis, revised rear aspect, and a number of other modifications, all helping to garner critical acclaim. And when TR2s entered into motorsports, with almost immediate success, the car's sporting image was further enhanced. The TR2 became a minor classic in its three years of production, and a major classic for collectors in later years. More importantly for Triumph, it gave the company a foothold in the budget sports car market and provided the basis for later successes in the TR range.

Racing first
(left) The TR2 competed in prestige races worldwide such as the Le Mans 24-hour and, as seen here, the 1955 Mille Miglia. Triumph's first works TR2 was entered into the previous year's race.

"The prototype TR2 was not only ugly, it was mechanically unsound. Chief tester Ken Richardson called the TR2's handling 'a bloody deathtrap.'"

Still loved
Though only around 8,600 TR2s came off the production line, they were received with immediate acclaim. Even today, there are clubs around the world dedicated to celebrating this most British car.

Tuning the TR2 – competition success

Despite being designed on a shoestring, the TR2 was very competitive. Soon after its launch a road-spec car managed 115 mph (185 km/h) at the Jabbeke Highway in Belgium, and a stripped-down version cracked a creditable 125 mph (201 km/h). The TR2's first competitive outing in 1954 yielded an outright win in the British RAC Rally driven by Johnny Wallwork. Another TR2 came 28th out of 365 starters in the Mille Miglia, "just driving beautifully and using only a quart of oil." Competition success was largely due to Ken Richardson's very stiff chassis design, which made tail-out cornering joyously predictable and easy to correct. Tweaking of the brakes, steering, and damper settings gave surprisingly sharp handling responses. Best of all, though, was that bombproof four-pot 2-liter engine with twin SU carbs, which could be really hammered and still run syrup-sweet.

Front view

Rear view

Side view

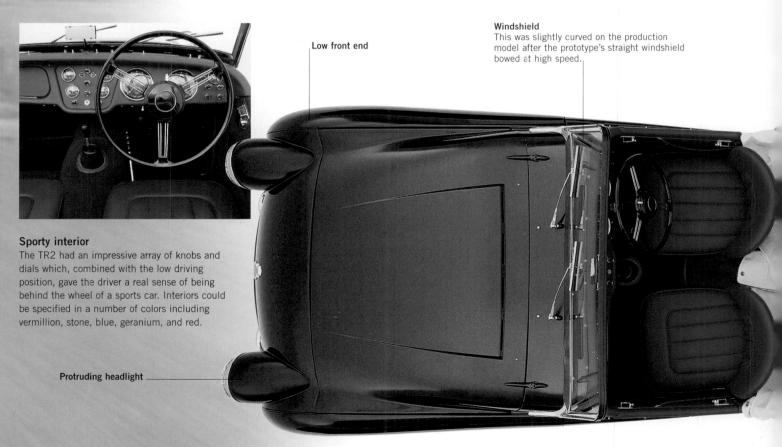

Windshield
This was slightly curved on the production model after the prototype's straight windshield bowed at high speed.

Low front end

Sporty interior
The TR2 had an impressive array of knobs and dials which, combined with the low driving position, gave the driver a real sense of being behind the wheel of a sports car. Interiors could be specified in a number of colors including vermillion, stone, blue, geranium, and red.

Protruding headlight

Design and Production

Model	Triumph TR2 (1953–55)
Production	8,628
Body style	Two-door, two-seater sports car.
Construction	Pressed-steel chassis with separate steel body.
Engine	Four-cylinder, overhead valve, 1991cc, twin SU carburetors.
Power output	90 bhp at 4800 rpm.
Transmission	Four-speed manual with Laycock overdrive option, initially on top gear only, then on top three (1955).
Suspension	Front: coil-spring and wishbone; Rear: live rear axle with semi-elliptic leaf springs.
Brakes	Lockheed hydraulic drums.
Max speed	105 mph (169 km/h)

Triumph followed its handsome but lifeless 1800/2000 roadsters with the butt-ugly TRX roadster prototype of 1950, but adverse public reaction an embarrassing electrical fire in front of Britain's Princess Margaret made them think again. The new TR2 project, codenamed 20TS, began in early '52 after a planned takeover of the Morgan company was rebuffed. With tight financial budgets, Triumph's second effort was loosely based on a 1936 Standard Flying Nine frame. Known as the TR1, it was slow, none too pretty, and handled like a pig. Their third attempt began in late '52, spawning the definitive TR2 of 1953. A stiff new chassis, independent coil front suspension, Vanguard-based engine, chunky lines, and top tilt of 100 mph (161 km/h) made it an instant hit. And with a basic price of around $800, the curvy TR2 made MG's TF look and feel like the pre-war antique it was.

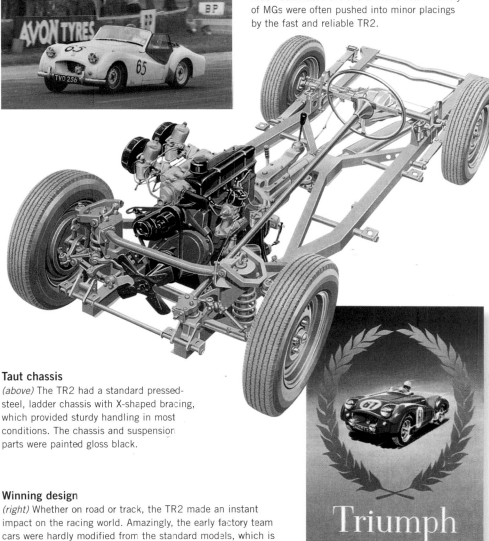

Beating the competition
(left) As well as competing in events abroad, TR2s also raced on British soil, where they pretty much dominated the sub-2-liter class. A variety of MGs were often pushed into minor placings by the fast and reliable TR2.

Taut chassis
(above) The TR2 had a standard pressed-steel, ladder chassis with X-shaped bracing, which provided sturdy handling in most conditions. The chassis and suspension parts were painted gloss black.

Winning design
(right) Whether on road or track, the TR2 made an instant impact on the racing world. Amazingly, the early factory team cars were hardly modified from the standard models, which is testament to the quality of the TR2's design.

Foldaway hood

Fuel filler-cap
The TR2 guzzled fuel pretty frugally – over 30 mpg (10.6 km/l).

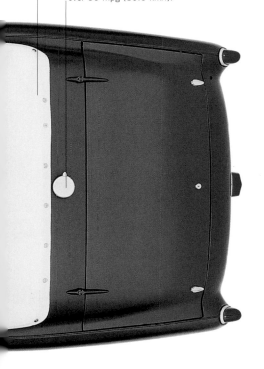

Triumph

CHEVROLET
CORVETTE

Like most of America, Harley Earl was impressed by European sports cars. He knew that there was no homegrown competition for the ever-successful Jaguars and Ferraris, but as GM's design chief he was in a position to do something about it. And he did, producing a two-seat sportster – the EX-122 – for the January 1953 Motorama. As initial reaction to the car was so favorable, a virtually unchanged Corvette started rolling off the Flint production line just five months later, and the first American sports car was born.

Early Corvettes were more show than go. The straight-six unit was slow and the cockpit cramped, but GM was also losing money on each one. Production for '53 stopped at about 300 cars; but while the company pondered the 'Vette's future, Ford unveiled its own two-seater, the T-Bird *(see pages 68–71)*. Faced with the prospect of losing out to its greatest rival, GM's doubts soon vanished and production went into overdrive. A vital option was offered in '54 – the V8 engine. Now with the grunt to match the looks, the 'Vette was an irresistible package, and it went from strength to strength.

Earl's baby
A wonderfully innovative piece of automotive styling, the first-generation Corvette reflects an era when the personal vision of one individual could be turned into a street-legal reality.

1954 Chevrolet Corvette

1963 Chevrolet Corvette Sting Ray

1968 Chevrolet Corvette Stingray

1978 Chevrolet Corvette   1984 Chevrolet Corvette

All-American hero
The 'Vette has gone from strength to strength, gaining weight along the way, but never losing its uniquely American personality. Its no-compromise attitude will probably ensure its survival for generations to come.

The first Corvette – an American sports car is born

The Corvette had an image problem at the outset because Chevrolet was derided by sports car enthusiasts as a manufacturer of dull family automobiles. The young Americans attracted to European sports models did not appreciate typical Chevy features such as Powerglide automatic transmission. With their rounded styling and pod-type taillights, the 1953–55 models also, in some people's view, fell short of classic looks. Uncertain of the market they were aiming at, Chevrolet advertisers initially played down the 'Vette's potential as a racer, emphasizing its "comfort and convenience." The Corvette was saved by the efforts of engineers Ed Cole and Zora Arkus-Duntov, who by 1956 had turned it into a really hot car, with a powerful V8 and a three-speed manual transmission. Only then did the publicity men promote the Corvette as "a genuine sports car with fiery performance."

Front view

Rear view

Side view

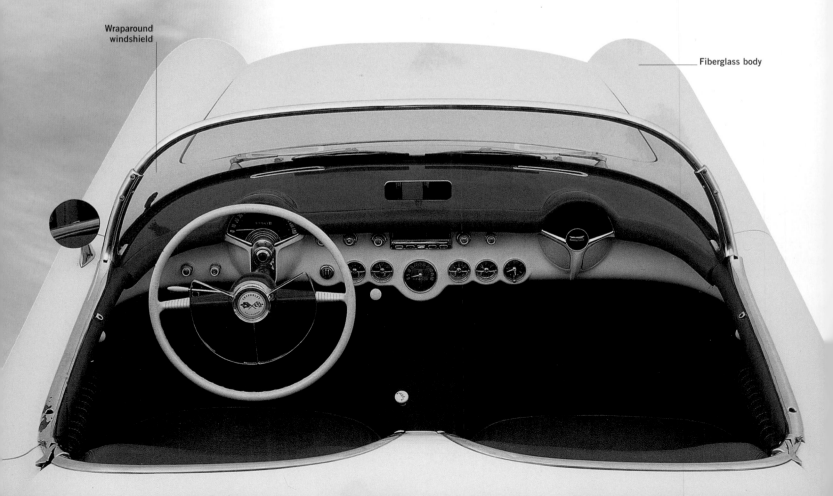

Wraparound windshield

Fiberglass body

Design and Production

Model	Chevrolet Corvette (1954)
Production	3,640
Body style	Two-door, two-seater sports.
Construction	Fiberglass body, steel chassis.
Engine	235.5cid straight-six.
Power output	150 bhp.
Transmission	Two-speed Powerglide automatic.
Suspension	Front: coil springs; Rear: leaf springs with live axle.
Brakes	Front and rear drums.
Max speed	107 mph (172 km/h)

The Corvette's novel fiberglass body was originally adopted as a practical measure, enabling GM to rush through an initial production run of 300 cars as quickly and economically as possible. Ironically, it proved to be the most durable feature of Corvettes through the following decades. Bodies were made by the Molded Fiber Glass Company of Ashtabula, Ohio, using the matched-metal die process. The total weight of the body parts was 340 lb (154 kg). The largest single piece was the underbody, to which the other panels were added in body assembly on a Chevrolet production line. As a company geared to mass production, Chevrolet had to learn to cope with making the more specialized Corvettes at a slower rhythm. It had, in the words of one executive, to "step out of its normal role of producing over 500 vehicles an hour, to make 500 specialized vehicles in, say, two weeks."

Public awareness
(left) As well as exhibiting at the Motoramas, GM promoted the Corvette through images like this '54 photo of 27 cars in Los Angeles. Within a couple of years, the 'Vette's profile had been further enhanced by high-profile wins at prestigious tracks such as Daytona and Sebring.

Plastic attraction
(right) The early 'Vette's fiberglass floorpan was light enough to be picked up with one hand, yet strong enough to withstand most kinds of impact.

Engine
(above) The 235cid straight-six was a tuned Blue Flame block with triple carburetors and higher compression, but it was still old and wheezy. As with virtually every other component on the '54 'Vette besides the body, the engine was standard Chevy stock, and it would be a year before a V8 transformed the model into a significant sportster.

Interior
(left) They may have looked good, but the row of dials spread right across the dashboard wasn't very practical, and it would take another four years before they were positioned in front of the driver.

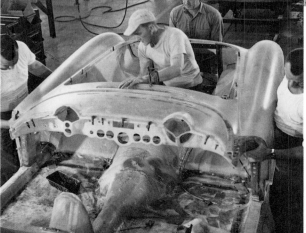

Assembly line
(left) The first Corvettes were manufactured at Chevy's plant in Flint, Michigan, but late in '53, production transferred to the larger GM facility in St. Louis. A further move in 1981 saw 'Vettes being built in Bowling Green, Kentucky, where they're still made today.

LANCIA
AURELIA B24 SPIDER

Lancia's new Aurelia was launched in 1950 as a replacement for its Aprilia model; but it wasn't until a year later that things got really exciting, when Pininfarina designed the B20 GT Coupe. Often credited as the first of the new breed of modern postwar GTs, the B20 incorporated a wonderfully free-revving unit that laid claim to being the world's first mass-produced V6. Another innovation was that the clutch and gearbox were housed in the transaxle, at the rear, to produce near-perfect weight distribution. Suspension wasn't exactly standard either, though it was typically Lancia; the Aurelia utilized front sliding pillars that Lancia had first employed in the 1920s. A series of engine upgrades ensued, accompanied by a number of other modifications, but the best was still to come in the form of the model unveiled at the 1955 Brussels Show – the B24 Spider.

Pininfarina's design team had created a lean beauty on top of a wheelbase shorter than previous Aurelias. The 2451cc engine may not have been the speediest powerplant around, but it was a smooth operator able to push out 118 bhp. And with the recent Lancia addition of De Dion rear suspension, it handled impeccably. A similar-looking convertible model replaced the Spider in '56, and this continued in production until 1958, though even by then less than 1,000 of both models had been produced. Today this rare and charismatic roadster is the most prized of the illustrious Aurelia family.

Unique to the Spider
(above) Though part of the Aurelia family, the Spider differed from the closed models in a number of ways, including the wraparound windshield and distinctive half-bumpers.

Engine note
The Spider may have been Pininfarina-designed, but its V6 was just as much of a talking point. And as you piled on the revs, the throbbing sound rose to a rich gurgle that was singularly tuneful from the twin exhausts.

The stylish B24 – Lancia's rare convertible

Lancia Aurelias performed well in racing in the early 1950s, notably the B20s with first in class at Le Mans in 1951 and in the Mille Miglia in 1952. But by the time the B24 Spider was introduced, the company had no money left for racing. In any case, the Spider was no red-hot racing roadster, but a car that offered a luxuriously smooth drive, with roadholding qualities that were spoken of with awe. The poor sales performance of the B24 did nothing to ease the financial difficulties besetting Lancia at this time. Owner Gianni Lancia was forced to sell off a majority holding in the company in 1957, the start of a slide that would end up with a takeover by Fiat. In all, 240 Spiders were built, and 521 of the subsequent B24 convertibles. The car's rarity only increased its appeal for those seduced by its outstanding qualities.

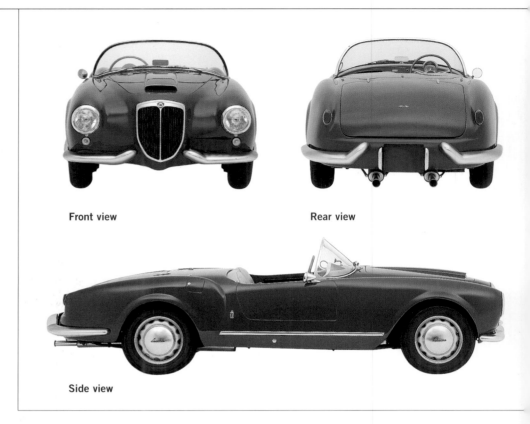

Front view   Rear view

Side view

Engine
The all-new 60° V6 started off at 1754cc in the B10, grew to 1991cc in the B21, then ballooned to the 2451cc of the B24 Spider. Power output had doubled by the time the last engine was introduced.

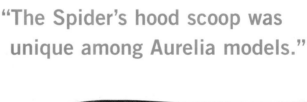

"The Spider's hood scoop was unique among Aurelia models."

Right hooker
Very few right-hand drive models were produced.

Design and Production

Model	Lancia Aurelia B24 Spider (1954–56)
Production	521
Body style	Two-seater sports convertible.
Construction	Monocoque with pressed-steel and box-section chassis frame.
Engine	Twin-overhead-valve aluminum alloy V6, 2451cc.
Power output	118 bhp at 5000 rpm.
Transmission	Four-speed manual.
Suspension	Front: Sliding pillar with beam axle and coil springs; Rear: De Dion axle on leaf springs.
Brakes	Hydraulic, finned alloy drums, inboard at rear.
Max speed	112 mph (180 km/h)

The Aurelia series began with a chassis developed by Vittorio Jano and a V6 engine designed by Francesco de Virgilio and Ettore Zaccone-Mina. What one car journalist described in 1956 as the "lithe, lovely, up-to-the-minute line" of the B24 Spider model was a credit to the styling house of Battista Pininfarina. The Spider was meant to impress Americans as the essence of European sophistication. Yet it failed to take the US by storm. Its looks and handling were appreciated, but potential customers were put off by a leaky top and cheap plastic side windows. In Pininfarina's original styling, there were no door handles to preserve the clean lines – leather twine inside the doors served the function. Handles were soon introduced as convenience won out over looks. Even the more comfortable but duller convertible failed to sell in sufficient numbers to keep production going beyond 1958.

Strange policy
(left) Left-hand drive, as on this Spider, would seem obvious for an Italian manufacturer, but up until the Aurelia, Lancia had eccentrically only built right-hand drive cars, even for the home market.

Happy union
(below) The flags of joint contributors Lancia and Pininfarina adorned the trunk.

Spacious boot

Interior
(above) The minimalist dashboard consisted of just three dials and a few switches. The Nardi steering wheel was standard on the Spider.

Style icon
(left) In addition to playing a major role in the styling of the Spider, Battista Pininfarina was also heavily involved in the model's actual production.

Seminal model
Launched as a stylish, personal sports compact, the Ford Thunderbird broke new ground in American car styling.

S·Y56

Maintaining standards
Still going strong after nearly 50 years, the T-Bird has won *Motor Trend*'s Car of the Year a record four times, with the most recent award in 2002.

1955 Ford Thunderbird

FORD
THUNDERBIRD

By the time the first Ford Thunderbird came off the production line at the end of 1954, it had already attracted huge publicity. After being unveiled at the Detroit Motor Show earlier that year, elements of the auto press were in rapture at the successful synergy of luxury and functionalism. It was all a big relief for Ford, who had seen Chevy's first Corvette *(see pages 60–63)* a few months before, and who now had to deliver an equally impressive model.

The T-Bird looked awesome and had the under-hood power to match. In top spec, the all-new 292cid V8 could speed the Thunderbird to 125 mph (201 km/h). Marilyn Monroe was one of a number of big names to own a first-generation T-Bird, but volume sales weren't materializing. The thing was, two-seaters just didn't sell in the predicted numbers, and by '58 the addition of rear seats meant that the Little Bird had become the Big Bird. Commercial considerations had forced the change, but at least the '55–'57 T-Bird was around long enough to establish itself as one of the great American design icons.

1959 Ford Thunderbird   1964 Ford Thunderbird   1966 Ford Thunderbird

The fabulous T-Bird – icon for a generation

Whether you regarded the handling of the early T-Birds as exciting kind of depended on what you were comparing them with. Coming from a standard contemporary Detroit-manufactured sedan, you might think the T-Bird cornered like a dream. If you had experience of European sports cars, on the other hand, its low-geared steering and soft springs gave what would seem an unimpressively wallowy effect. What the Thunderbird definitely did have was power. The original Mercury-sourced Y-block 292cid V8 gave an output upward of 200 bhp, powering acceleration up to 60 mph (96 km/h) in under 10 seconds. By 1957, you could buy a T-Bird with a supercharged 312cid engine generating 300 bhp. Despite the power and the racy name, the Thunderbird remained more of a stylish "personal car" than a real sports car – but was, for all that, no less of a classic.

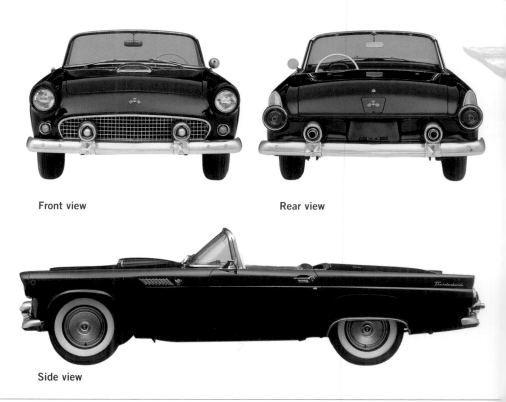

Front view

Rear view

Side view

Design and Production

Model	Ford Thunderbird (1955)
Production	16,155 (1955)
Body style	Two-door, two-seater convertible.
Construction	Steel body and chassis.
Engine	292cid V8.
Power output	193 bhp.
Transmission	Three-speed manual with optional overdrive, optional three-speed Ford-O-Matic automatic.
Suspension	Front: independent coil springs; Rear: leaf springs with live axle.
Brakes	Front and rear drums.
Max speed	105–125 mph (169–201 km/h)

Ford stylist Bill Boyer is usually credited with the clean, aerodynamic lines of the 1955-57 T-Birds. The fins, bumpers, and chromework were strikingly modest by the standards of the decade, although the 1957 model developed towards a less restrained look in response to the taste of the American public. The Thunderbird was Ford's response to Chevrolet's Corvette, based on the same calculation – backed up by market research – that there might be an untapped demand in the US for a homegrown two-seater sports car. From a business point of view, Ford did a better job of tapping this market, putting out a car with a lot of power for a very reasonable price – initially under $3,000. T-Birds easily outsold Corvettes, with 54,000 of the two-seaters built over three years. But a telling Ford publicity shot of 1957 shows a family of four squashed into the two-seater, with kids squeezed in between their parents. There simply wasn't enough demand for two-seaters, and the four-seat Thunderbird, logically introduced by Ford in 1958, predictably outsold its predecessor.

Stamp of approval
(below) The T-Bird soon became a symbol of American Fifties utopia. As this stamp from the South Pacific illustrates, its influence spread further afield than just the shores of the US.

Wide appeal
(above) Ford was eager to market the T-Bird wider than just the young, single male. Advertising such as this depicted the car being driven by couples as well as families with children, though they would have found it a tight fit squeezing into the Little Bird.

Engine
(above) The T-Bird's monster Mercury 292cid V8 was made from cast iron and could push out 193 bhp with the manual box and an extra five horses if buyers chose automatic transmission. It came with a four-barrel Holley carburetor and twin exhausts.

Creature comforts
(left) The dash may have been fairly minimal, with just a high-level speedo and tachometer to keep the driver amused, but there were a plethora of options available. You could power-assist almost everything, though the most expensive extra was the push-button radio; at $100 it cost more than power steering.

Promoting the T-Bird
(right) The T-Bird was exhibited at numerous car shows, here displayed at the London Motor Show. Among celebrity owners of the '55-'57 model were actresses Debbie Reynolds and Marilyn Monroe.

ALFA ROMEO
GIULIETTA SPIDER

In 1957 $6,577 (£2,349) bought an Alfa Giulietta Spider or a Jaguar MKI and an MGA *(see pages 76–79)*. Incredibly expensive, the gem-like Alfa set new standards of refinement and performance in an era when many sports cars were damp, drafty, and as dull as dirt. At last, here was an open car with roll-up windows, a roomy cabin, and a simple top that didn't take till the end of the downpour to raise. But what made the Giulietta so amazing was that gorgeous Pininfarina styling. A combination of refined elegance and stylish impudence, it ranks as one of the most handsome of all postwar Alfas.

Hardtop Giuliettas may have earned laurels on the track, but the Spider was more at home in Hollywood and St. Tropez – it was just too pretty to race. Playboys and starlets beat a path to Alfa showrooms, desperate to own the best-looking car of the decade. Scores of feature movie appearances followed and nobody seemed to care that the little Alfa cost more than a Jag XK150, AC Ace, or Jensen 541, or three times the price of a Morgan Plus Four. Pretty enough to stop a speeding train, it handled better than most other sports cars and could knock on the door of 110 mph (177 km/h) – and all from 1300cc. Perhaps London's *Daily Express* summed the Giulietta Spider's appeal best of all: "This impeccable convertible is a dream of delight for today's gilded youth."

At the races
(right) Though Stuart Lewis-Evans drove for Aston Martin at the 1958 Le Mans 24-hour, his support crew used a Giulietta Spider as their trackside runaround.

Making a mark
Before the Giulietta, Alfa Romeo had been a name associated more with race cars than road vehicles, but the new model propelled the company into big-time mass production.

Winning combo
(below, below left) The Spider was a joy to look at and a pleasure to drive. Years of Grand Prix racing experience helped to create a supremely balanced car.

Alfa's sexy Spider – sleek Italian styling

The Alfa Giulietta was that exceptional phenomenon, an all-new car. From the engine and transmission through the axle and suspensions to the body and styling, it was originated with an uncompromising eye to quality. The small but powerful four-cylinder engine, with two chain-driven overhead camshafts and a rigid five-bearing crankshaft, proved to be an instant classic, and variants were to power Alfas through to the 1970s. An all-synchromesh four-speed transmission, coil-spring front suspension, and bevel rear axle contributed to the quality of the driving experience. The first model of the Giulietta series was introduced in 1954. Appearing in 1957, the Spider was a relative latecomer, but held its own for looks alongside the Sprint coupé of the previous year. Considering the breathtaking price tag, the 14,300 Spiders sold represented an impressive achievement.

Front view

Rear view

Side view

Engine
The 1290cc engine featured a double overhead cam and aluminum castings. While displacement remained the same, power output grew progressively through using different carburetor and tweaking compression ratios.

Spider Veloce scoop
Air scoop was to accommodate dual Weber carburetor.

Design and Production

Model	Alfa Romeo Giulietta Spider (1954–62)
Production	14,300
Body style	Two-seater convertible.
Construction	Steel monocoque.
Engine	1290cc four-cylinder.
Power output	90 bhp.
Transmission	Four-speed manual.
Suspension	Front: independent coil springs; Rear: trailing arms with coil springs.
Brakes	Drums all around.
Max speed	100 mph (161 km/h)

The Giulietta series were the cars that transformed Alfa Romeo into a quantity manufacturer and a major player in the Italian auto industry. Whereas in the early 1950s the company's 1900 Sprint had been thought of as a great success with sales of around 17,000, Alfa built an astounding 178,000 of all kinds of Giulietta in little over a decade. This required, among other things, the replacement of the company's old Portello works in Milan with a vast new factory outside the city at Arese. The key to the Giulietta's phenomenal commercial success was the sheer glamor of the four-seater Bertone-styled Sprint coupé and the convertible two-seater Spider styled by Pininfarina – along with their even racier derivatives such as the Sprint Speciale and Sprint Zagato. Racing and rallying successes were a secondary but useful boost to a reputation that was founded above all on style. The prestige of both the Sprint and Spider rubbed off on the less elegant four-door sedan Giuliettas that became Alfa's bread-and-butter product.

Big in the US
(left) Many Giuliettas such as this 1960 example found their way to the US thanks to the efforts of Max Hoffman, the famed car importer. Dual-carb Veloce Spiders are known as Super Spiders in the US.

Tidy top
The top tucked neatly away behind the seats.

Shorter model
The Spider's wheelbase was 1.97 in (50 mm) shorter than the original Sprint.

Checkered flag
(right) With their fantastic handling capabilities and great engines, Giuliettas were more than competent race cars, notching up notable victories worldwide. Here B.C. McCann wins a 10-lap race in Louisiana.

Adaptable Alfa
(below) The joys of open-top driving were plain to see in Alfa's literature for the Spider. In addition to the fabric top, a Pininfarina-designed plastic version could be ordered.

transformability

Test car
A preproduction MGA, known as the EX182, sits by the track at Silverstone, with Ken Wharton behind the wheel. The bodies of these prototypes were constructed from aluminum.

MGA

"The new MGA's aerodynamic design was a radical departure from the boxy profile of the pre-war T Series."

Although MG's T Series *(see pages 24–27)* had been a winner for the company, there was little doubt that by 1955, it was reaching the end of its natural life. Sales of the traditional-looking TF were flagging, and many thought it was time for the range to receive an overhaul. Enter the MGA. With its sleek design and all-new B-Series engine, MG really had come up with the goods. The transmission was another recent development, and the MGA's chassis had been specially adapted from the TD Midget. Combined with a sensible pricing policy that meant it was cheaper than its Triumph TR3 and Austin-Healey 100 *(see pages 116–19)* rivals, it all added up to an attractive package. And with an impressive 13,000 sold in its first year, the buying public obviously thought so too.

The omens were good even before the September '55 launch. MG had entered three prototypes into Le Mans and two of them finished in creditable fifth and sixth positions in their class. So not only was there a brand-spanking-new production model on the table that looked good and was eminently affordable, but buyers were purchasing a car with a proven sporting pedigree. Twin-cam and 1600cc engines followed, as did disc brakes, and MG had made the successful transition to becoming a manufacturer of "modern" sports cars. Needless to say, Americans bought them by the truckload, and by the time the MGA moved aside for the MGB in 1962, around 81,000 had found homes in American driveways.

Myriad of options
With a removable hardtop available as an option, in addition to "real" windows instead of the standard soft sidescreens, it was no surprise that the MGA was such a hit with buyers seeking a car with a sense of all-around roadgoing fun.

"A" for effort – MG's path to modernity

"Racy looks. Racy performance. Supreme stability. Superb stopping power. Plus superb craftsmanship..." That was how the MG publicity blurb (maybe a little strapped for fresh adjectives) summed up the appeal of the 1600 version of the MGA in 1961. By then, the public had had plenty of time to adjust to the radical modernization of MG's image from the essentially prewar look of the T-series, the MGA's famous predecessors. The novelty of the MGA was much more a matter of style than substance. Under the shapely exterior lay a robust, heavy chassis and conventional suspension. Many of the parts were standard Austin or Morris components – since MG was part of BMC, formed when the two big companies merged in 1952. In terms of speed and style, the car essentially sold itself, especially in the US, which took around four-fifths of all MGAs.

Front view

Rear view

Side view

Handle-free
The uncluttered design meant the MGA was designed without door handles.

Hand-pressed steel panels

Luggage rack

Trunk space
The shallow trunk contained the spare wheel and meant limited space for luggage.

Design and Production

Model	MGA (1955–62)
Production	101,081
Body styles	Two-door sports coupé and convertible.
Construction	Steel.
Engines	Four-cylinder 1489cc, 1588cc, 1622cc (Twin Cam).
Power output	72 bhp, 79.5 bhp, 85 bhp.
Transmission	Four-speed manual.
Suspension	Front: independent; Rear: leaf spring.
Brakes	Rear drums, front discs. All discs on De Luxe and twin-cam.
Max speed	100 mph (161 km/h); 113 mph (181 km/h) (Twin-cam)

The MG TF, which the A supplanted on the production line at the Abingdon, England, plant, had a coach-built bod with wood frames. So it was something of a revolution for the company to make the MGA's body entirely from pressed-steel panels. The car's separate box-section chassis was extremely strong, although some thought it was achieved at the expense of too much weight. The original MGA 1500 was succeeded in 1959 by the 1600, which had a 1588cc instead of 1489cc engine and front-wheel disc brakes to cope with the extra oomph. The 1622cc-engined MkII followed in 1961. A choice of convertible or coupe versions was always offered. Between 1958 and 1960, there was also a twin-cam MGA in production, the fastest of the series with a top speed of 110 mph (177 km/h). Only 2,000 of these were built, however, out of a total of 101,081 MGAs of all kinds manufactured between 1955 and 1962.

Brochure cover
(*left*) The byline on the cover of the sales brochure for the MGA 1600 said "Safety Fast," referring to the A's new 79.5 bhp engine and the addition of front disc brakes. The "superb stopping power" also included improved linings on the rear brakes.

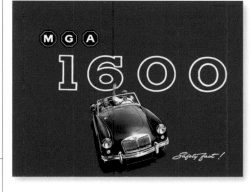

Tail end
(*right*) MG proudly stated in its brochure that "this is the view of the MGA 1600 that other motorists see most often – the sleek, streamlined, sculptured tail that frequently disappears out of sight as swiftly as the car comes into view."

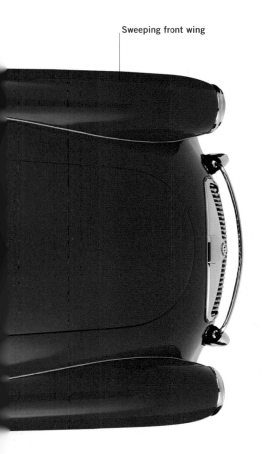

Sweeping front wing

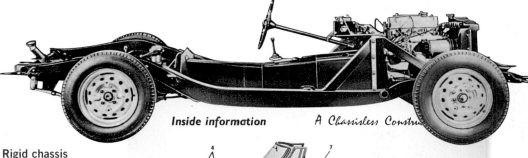

Inside information   *A Chassisless Constru...*

Rigid chassis
(*above*) The MGA's box section chassis was strong and provided the car with a low center of gravity.

Later underpinnings
(*right*) The MGB that followed incorporated unitary construction instead of the A's separate chassis.

1. Lockheed hydraulic front disc brakes, self-adjusting, employing 10¾ in. (27·3 cm.) discs.
2. Direct rack and pinion steering (2·9 turns from lock to lock) gives finger-tip control.
3. Highly efficient twin air cleaners and silencers to quieten engine air intake.
4. Twin S.U. semi-downdraught carburetters fed

6. New-type Borg & Beck 'diaphragm spring' clutch reduces pedal effort and driver fatigue.
7. Conveniently placed ratchet-type hand brake between bucket seats.
8. Easy-to-hand central gear change lever for four-speed gearbox with synchromesh on second, third, and top. Overdrive optional.

MERCEDES
190SL

For years enthusiasts saw the Mercedes 190SL as something for the women, preferring instead the faster 300SL. But these days the dainty 190 roadster has become something of an icon. Based on the underpinnings of the 190 Ponton sedan, the baby SL was launched at the Geneva Motor Show in 1954, and it was the first stage in Mercedes' quest to build the best sports car in the world.

Overengineered, overweight, and underpowered, the 190SL was no great performer, but it shared the 300SL's distinctive wheelarch treatment, looked very ritzy, and was beautifully detailed. Most went to the US, where owners weren't bothered by the glacial performance and uninspired handling. Mercedes did little to update the 190, and it was quietly dropped in 1963. But since then prices of 190SLs have been edging up, and the 300SL's baby sister is finally enjoying something of a renaissance.

190 on celluloid
(below) Among the many movie cameos made by the 190 was this one with Frank Sinatra and Grace Kelly in *High Society* (1956).

Off-screen star
(below right) The 190 had a number of celebrity owners including Yul Brynner, here taking a break from filming *Solomon and Sheba* (1959).

Appreciating classic
With its distinctive '50s shape, the 190SL is now one of the most sought-after postwar classic Mercedes.

The classy 190 – luxury sports cruiser

The 190SL was based on the sedan engineering of the Mercedes 180, with its unit-construction pressed-steel body and chassis. The suspension was also derived from the same source. The rear swing-axle could have caused problems for drivers if they had been inclined to push the car to the extreme limits of its performance, but this was essentially a car for people who wanted the feel of power in reserve, rather than living on the edge. You could in principle remove the fold-away top and the bumpers to give the 190SL a "sports roadster" look, but it is doubtful that anyone did. More to the point for the 190SL image were the reclining leather seats, the cigar-lighter and glareproof rearview mirror, and the lockable glove compartment. This was a car to wear jewelry in. It looked and felt as expensive as it was, and that was what really counted.

Front view

Rear view

Side view

Interior
Standard fare included an oil pressure gauge, reading light, and a super-efficient heater. Buyers could choose from a number of upholstery schemes.

Design and Production

Model	Mercedes 190SL (1955–63)
Production	25,881
Body style	Two-seater convertible.
Construction	Steel body with separate chassis.
Engine	1897cc four-cylinder.
Power output	120 bhp.
Transmission	Four-speed manual.
Suspension	Front: independent with coil spring; Rear: independent with coil spring.
Brakes	Drums all around.
Max speed	107 mph (172 km/h)

In contrast to its high-performance contemporary, the 300SL, the Mercedes 190SL was more of an upmarket touring car than an outright sports car. Publicity material for the 190SL was aimed squarely at the self-satisfied image of its clientele. "Whenever you stroll with your elegant car along the avenues or boulevards." a Mercedes brochure told them, "admiring looks follow your way and you almost hear people say: 'You have chosen intelligently and with good taste.'" Comfort and safety were better selling points than performance. Mercedes was eager that its customers appreciate the car's "superior road ability" and the slim, two-spoke steering wheel that "feels so well in your hands." If Mercedes-Benz left the car virtually unchanged through a decade of production, this is probably because it fulfilled so well its solid role in reestablishing the company's international position in the postwar world.

Extra space
An "emergency" seat could be put in behind the front seats.

Mercedes luggage
One luxury extra on offer was a set of suitcases that fit perfectly into the trunk.

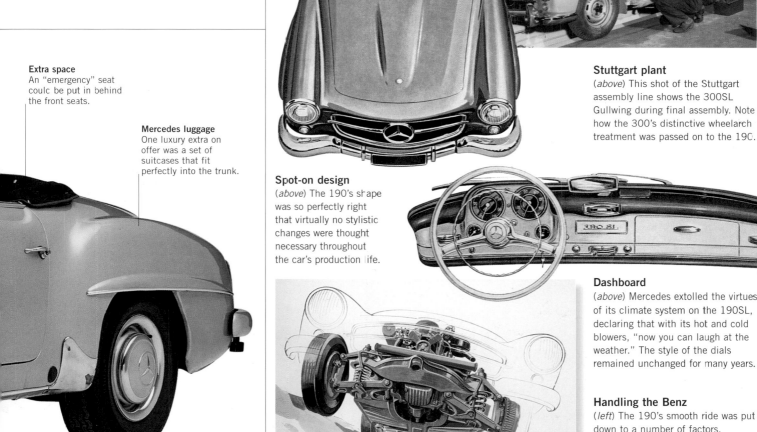

Stuttgart plant
(*above*) This shot of the Stuttgart assembly line shows the 300SL Gullwing during final assembly. Note how the 300's distinctive wheelarch treatment was passed on to the 190.

Spot-on design
(*above*) The 190's shape was so perfectly right that virtually no stylistic changes were thought necessary throughout the car's production life.

Dashboard
(*above*) Mercedes extolled the virtues of its climate system on the 190SL, declaring that with its hot and cold blowers, "now you can laugh at the weather." The style of the dials remained unchanged for many years.

Handling the Benz
(*left*) The 190's smooth ride was put down to a number of factors, including independent suspension, use of a single-joint swing axle, and the car's low center of gravity.

BMW 507

By the early 1950s, BMW had established a reputation for innovative engineering, with an emphasis on motorcycle manufacturing. Though the company had produced a number of notable cars – the Mille Millia-winning 328 *(see pages 32–35)* was one of the seminal models of the 1930s – it was two wheels instead of four that were grabbing most of the headlines – until the stunning 507. Unveiled at the 1955 Frankfurt Show, it had looks to die for and should really have been a best-seller. Instead, by the time the last of the mere 252 (possibly 253) cars rolled off the production line in 1959, the model had almost bankrupted the company. The problem was that the car that looked like a million dollars almost cost as much. Quite simply, BMW priced the car way too high. Maybe it was to cover the cost of hiring Albrecht Goertz to pen the 507's gorgeous lines, or it could even have been to address BMW's dire postwar financial position. Whatever the reason, the bottom line was that the 507 leaked money like no other model in the company's history.

On a purely aesthetic level, the 507's sleek, understated design made it a real head-turner. Under the hood, the 3.2-liter V8 sped the roadster to a claimed 138 mph (222 km/h) and though it was no match for the contemporary Mercedes 300SL, it was certainly no slouch. A disaster, then, for BMW, but a true gem for connoisseurs of automotive art who may agree that no superlatives can describe this glorious burst of creativity from the usually austere Germans.

The King's Beemer
Elvis Presley was a keen car fan and among his collection was this 507, acquired while stationed in Frankfurt in 1956.

Timeless design
Looking at the 507,
you can see where
BMW designers got
their inspiration for the
current Z8 roadster.

A beautiful baby – poorly managed

BMW was struggling in the 1950s to recover from the disaster of World War II, which had ended with the company's Berlin and Eisenach factories now out of reach behind the Iron Curtain. The unveiling of the 507 was a calculated move to reenter the expensive and risky sports car field to which the company had so notably contributed in the 1930s with the 328. The exclusivity of the 507 was guaranteed by its price; in the US it retailed for almost $9,000, approaching triple the price of a Corvette. Overpricing made the car a perfect glamor flagship for BMW, but a sales disaster. The number of 507s sold – a few hundred in three years – might have been impressive and financially viable in the hand-built days of the 1930s, when sports cars often sold in dozens instead of hundreds. But in the age of the production line it sadly made no economic sense.

Front view

Rear view

Side view

Interior
As well as an adjustable steering wheel, the 507 had a number of innovations that would become standard on other cars, including internally-adjustable side mirrors. The two main dials on the dash were a tachometer and a speedometer.

German similarities
The 507 bore a resemblance to the contemporary Mercedes 300SL roadster.

Brakes
Most cars came with drum brakes, but some later models had discs.

Design and Production

Model	BMW 507 (1956–59)
Production	252/3, most LHD
Body style	Two-seater roadster.
Construction	Box section and tubular steel chassis; aluminum body.
Engine	All-aluminum 3168cc V8, two valves per cylinder.
Power output	150 bhp at 5000 rpm; some later cars 160 bhp at 5600 rpm.
Transmission	Four-speed manual.
Suspension	Front: unequal-length wishbones, torsion-bar springs and telescopic shocks; Rear: live axle, torsion-bar springs.
Brakes	Drums front and rear; front discs and rear drums on later cars.
Max speed	125 mph (201 km/h); 135–140 mph (217–225 km/h) with optional 3.42:1 final drive.

In its bid to create a supercar to compete with the Mercedes 300SL, BMW commissioned German aristocrat Count Albrecht Goertz – the man who would later create the immensely successful Datsun 240Z – to provide the style. Goertz produced his supremely elegant look for the 507 in consultation with the American importer of BMWs, Max Hoffman. Beautifully crafted in light alloy, it created exactly the stunning impact BMW desired.

To supply the power, BMW depended on a high-compression version of its existing 3200cc V8 engine. BMW boasted in its promotional literature for the 507 that in its production "machine and assembly lines are given only those tasks that properly belong to modern mass production." This half-hearted embrace of quantity production methods – the 507's body was coach-built – contributed to the car's superb finish but inevitably raised costs and lowered output.

Adaptable roofing
(left) An all-weather top came as standard, but the 507 was offered with a removable coupé top to "accentuate the racy elegance of the car." This brochure image extols the car's fine lines, which were undeniably gorgeous.

Windshield
A half-width racing windshield was available as an optional extra.

Air-bay vent

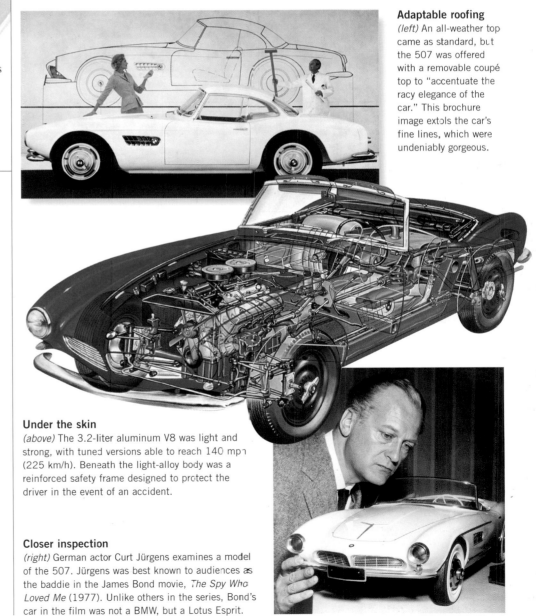

Under the skin
(above) The 3.2-liter aluminum V8 was light and strong, with tuned versions able to reach 140 mph (225 km/h). Beneath the light-alloy body was a reinforced safety frame designed to protect the driver in the event of an accident.

Closer inspection
(right) German actor Curt Jürgens examines a model of the 507. Jürgens was best known to audiences as the baddie in the James Bond movie, *The Spy Who Loved Me* (1977). Unlike others in the series, Bond's car in the film was not a BMW, but a Lotus Esprit.

AC ACE-BRISTOL

The AC Ace was designed by John Tojeiro, and when released in 1953 had an immediate impact. Its elegant looks and uncomplicated mechanics attracted enormous attention, so much so that the Ace went on to provide the platform for the legendary AC Cobra *(see pages 148–51)*. Even without the addition of a 7-liter engine, the original Ace had respectable enough performance figures with its 1991cc AC block, but there was a feeling that the light alloy body deserved something a bit livelier.

The answer came in 1956 when AC equipped Bristol's 1971cc straight-six into the Ace. This classic powerplant was a real gem and added an extra 35 horses to the 85 bhp AC unit. A later option was a lusty 2.6-liter Ford Zephyr engine, but purists argue that the Bristol-powered version is the real thoroughbred Ace. Whatever the block, the Ace's timeless design has guaranteed it a place in driving annals.

Steep incline
The Ace competed in all kinds of events including international hill climbs as seen here in 1956.

1959 racer
Silverstone was a favorite track for the Ace's zesty Bristol powerplant.

Warming the pedals
Open-top driving could be a
bleak affair in some climates,
but a tonneau cover was
available for die-hards who
always drove with the top
down. It kept your feet warm
while your face froze.

The select Ace – a very British sports car

The introduction of the Bristol engine in the AC Ace in 1956 was an inevitable response to the model's success, which led to a search for a modern engine to match the modern design. Ironically, the 2-liter six-cylinder Bristol was itself derived from the unit that had powered the prewar BMW 328 *(see pages 32–35)*, though it had been extensively developed over the years. AC Bristols were produced until 1961, when Bristol stopped supplying the engines, having decided to change over to more powerful Chrysler V8s in its own cars. The AC Bristol was no slouch, with a maximum speed of 117 mph (188 km/h), and it proved an effective competitor in many forms of motorsport. But its performance was retrospectively put in the shade by its successor. In 1963, the Ace evolved into the electrifying AC Cobra *(see pages 148–51)* – and that was, as they say, another story.

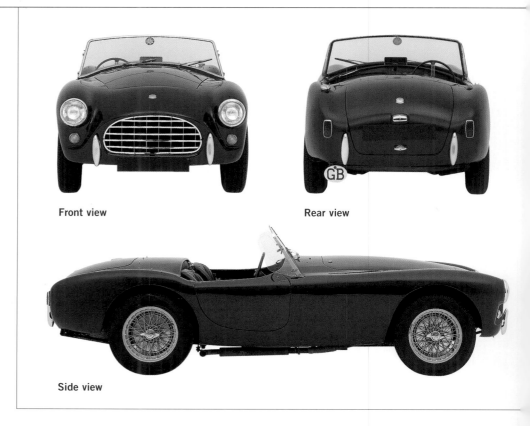

Front view

Rear view

Side view

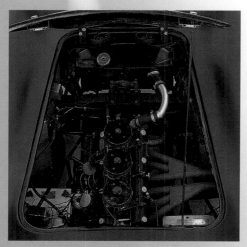

Engine
The hardy Bristol straight-six had been around for a few years by the time it was used in the Ace, and would continue in production through into the Sixties. Tuned versions could push out 128 bhp.

"AC was one of the oldest British carmakers, nicknamed 'the Savile Row of motordom'."

Hood lock
Two chrome latches allowed access to the engine.

Superleggera construction
Aluminum steel panels covered a network of steel tubes.

Design and Production

Model	AC Ace-Bristol (1956–61)
Production	463
Body style	Two-door, two-seat sports roadster.
Construction	Space-frame chassis, light alloy body.
Engine	Six-cylinder push-rod 1971cc.
Power output	105 bhp at 5000 rpm (optional high performance output of 128 bhp at 5750 rpm).
Transmission	Four-speed manual Bristol (optional overdrive).
Suspension	Independent front and rear with transverse leaf spring and lower wishbones.
Brakes	Front and rear drums. Front discs from 1957.
Max speed	117 mph (188 km/h)

AC was a small company based in Thames Ditton, southwest of London – a survivor that had started by making three-wheeled delivery vehicles for butchers before World War I and was later sustained by a contract to provide motorized invalid carriages for Britain's Ministry of Health. AC also had a tradition of producing handsome sports cars, using a 1991cc overhead camshaft straight-six engine. This had first been introduced way back in 1919, and had been successfully upgraded over the years. The Ace was created by matching this traditional unit with a thoroughly modern welded steel-tube "ladder" chassis, with independent transverse-leaf suspension all around, sourced in from John Tojeiro. The shapely light alloy body was shamelessly Ferrari-influenced, and all the better for it. The open-top Ace sports car of 1953 was joined a year later by the Aceca sports coupe version. The Bristol-engined version was available from 1956, and a Ford Zephyr-engined version from 1961. Of the 1,057 Aces and Acecas that were made at Thames Ditton by the time production was halted in 1963, 635 had the Bristol engine. Only 43 were equipped with the Zephyr powerplant.

Luggage locker
The small trunk was expanded on later Aces.

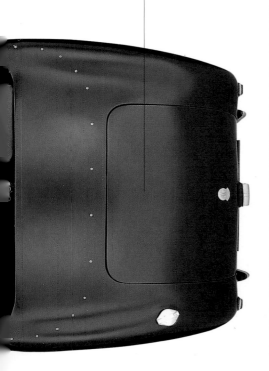

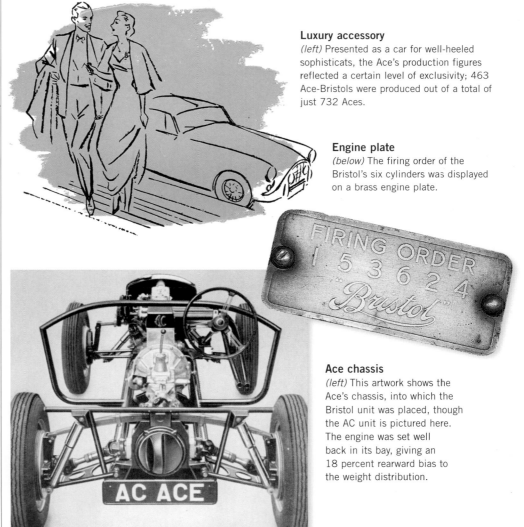

Luxury accessory
(left) Presented as a car for well-heeled sophisticats, the Ace's production figures reflected a certain level of exclusivity; 463 Ace-Bristols were produced out of a total of just 732 Aces.

Engine plate
(below) The firing order of the Bristol's six cylinders was displayed on a brass engine plate.

FIRING ORDER
1 5 3 6 2 4
Bristol

Ace chassis
(left) This artwork shows the Ace's chassis, into which the Bristol unit was placed, though the AC unit is pictured here. The engine was set well back in its bay, giving an 18 percent rearward bias to the weight distribution.

AC ACE

AUSTIN-HEALEY
FROGEYE SPRITE MKI

Welcome to the wonderful world of the Austin-Healey Sprite MkI, one of the quirkiest offerings ever to come out of Britain. After having successfully pitched the Austin-Healey 100 into the large sports car market, it was decided to develop a smaller model, using components from other British Motor Corporation (BMC) cars to save costs. The resulting Sprite MkI was released in 1958 with numerous parts from the Austin A35 as well as the Morris Minor's steering rack. One unique aspect was the Sprite's bulbous headlights, positioned in such a way as to earn the model its "Frogeye" nickname. Along with the smiling grille and petite dimensions, it all added up to a seriously cute car. And the buying public thought so, too, with just under 50,000 MkI Sprites produced. The majority went to the US, where it is known as the "Bugeye."

Though the Sprite name lived on until 1971, and the car itself became the basis for the MG Midget, the original "Frogeye" ceased production in 1961 when the MkII – with a restyled front end – was introduced. By this time, the sprightly Sprite – it was also praised for its lively engine and firm handling – had already become a cult classic. And with one of the most endearing faces in automotive history, it's easy to see why.

Road and track
The Sprite's solid ride and spirited engine made it not only a true enthusiasts' car, but also a popular club racer.

Sports star
Race car driver Stirling Moss recognized the Sprite's sporty appeal and drove one in a number of events.

The bold Sprite – bug-eyed driving

Small and compact, the Sprite was described by Austin boss Sir Leonard Lord as the kind of car "that a chap could keep in his bike shed." And not only chaps: it was the first sports car sold in large numbers to women drivers. The Sprite's selling points were economy, practicality, and, above all, fun. It did not offer a high level of comfort. In early models, if you had chosen a heater as an optional extra, you had to stop the car and open the hood to turn it on or off. Promotional literature stressed that the upholstery was "hard-wearing and washable" – it certainly wasn't luxurious. The standard 948cc BMC engine gave adequate, instead of exciting, performance, but a variety of super-tuned versions were produced that raced with considerable success in the hands of Stirling and Pat Moss, among others.

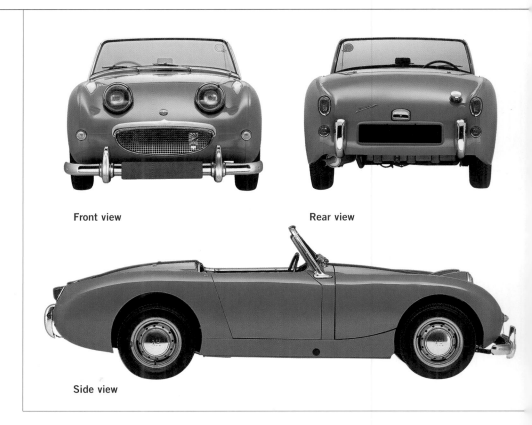

Front view

Rear view

Side view

"The Frogeye combined a simplicity of design with pert looks – the perfect recipe for a cult classic."

Easy access
Rear-hinged hood allowed easy engine access.

Snug cockpit
There was not much room for anything but the two occupants.

Engine
The A-Series 948cc unit came from the Austin A35 sedan, part of BMC's brief to build a sports model as cheaply as possible. The Sprite version had some modifications, including the fitting of twin SU carburetors.

Design and Production

Model	Austin-Healey Frogeye Sprite MkI (1958–61)
Production	49,500 (est.)
Body style	Two-seater roadster.
Construction	Unitary body/chassis.
Engine	BMC A–Series 948cc, four-cylinder, overhead valve.
Power output	43 bhp at 5200 rpm.
Transmission	Four-speed manual, synchromesh on top three ratios.
Suspension	Front: independent, coil springs and wishbones; Rear: quarter-elliptic leaf springs, rigid axle.
Brakes	Hydraulic, drums all around.
Max speed	84 mph (135 km/h)

Designed by Healey's Gerry Coker, the Sprite was not only fun to drive, but looked like fun. The bug-eye headlights were a lucky accident when retracting headlights were rejected by BMC on the grounds of cost. The use of standard BMC components – including the Austin A35 engine, transmission, and front suspension – made the Sprite practical, with spares widely available, and cheap. Selling for ($1,900) £690, it was about half the price of most other sports cars. After Healey had come up with a prototype, development and assembly of the Sprite were transferred to the factory of rival MG – both Austin and MG were now under the BMC umbrella. The car was of pressed-steel construction, with an underframe from Thompson Pressings welded to a superstructure made by the Pressed Steel Company. In total, 130,000 cars bearing the Sprite name were built, 50,000 of them original "Frogeye" Sprites.

Aspirational advertising
(right) The artwork adorning the sales brochure, with a pipe-smoking character chatting to his well-heeled companions, reinforced the idea of the Sprite as an expensive British sports model. Yet with a price tag of just ($1,035) £660, it was affordable enough to be bought by car enthusiasts from all classes.

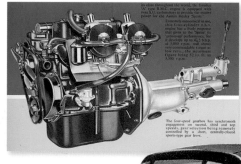

Interior
Everything was within reach, with the speedometer on the right and the tachometer on the left.

Power unit
(left) The engine offered "grown-up" performance and was linked to a four-speed transmission that was controlled by a "sports-type" gear stick.

Flexible protection
(above) The detachable hood and sidescreens were coated in plastic and could be stored behind the seats.

Production line
(right) The Sprite was manufactured at MG's plant in Abingdon, England, where other larger Healeys were also produced.

Housewife's favorite
More upmarket than a Frogeye Sprite
(see pages 92–95) or MGA (see pages
76–79), the Alpine became a suburban
women's favorite with the style and
image of a little Jaguar.

Series II

SUNBEAM
ALPINE

Like most British car companies of the late '50s, the Rootes Group knew that the American market would buy every low, sporty, two-seater it could make. With boatloads of MGs and Triumphs heading Stateside, the Coventry firm decided to join the fray and build a new Sunbeam sports car. But in typical Rootes style its new Alpine was nothing more than yesterday's lunch warmed over. Apart from the voguish rear fins, the chassis was culled from the Hillman Husky wagon and the running gear was pure Sunbeam Rapier.

Technically undistinguished, the Alpine's greatest strengths were those trendy fins and British bloodline. Finely detailed, with the option of whitewall tires, wire wheels, and snug hardtop, the Alpine initially sold surprisingly well. But by 1963 the Alpine's reign as the drop-top darling of the masses came to an end with the faster, better handling, and more modern MGB *(see pages 132–35)*. It left the Alpine to be remembered as "that nice little sports job for the little lady."

The Alpine's lifespan
A range of facelifts followed the original Series I, with the fins trimmed in '64 and a decent 1725cc engine added in '65. Production stopped with the Series V of 1968.

Series III   Series IV

Series V

The popular Alpine – a simple sportster

Rootes Group marketing men were clearly happy with the "Alpine" name they had used for their 1953 Sunbeam–Talbot two-seater, since they kept it for the different model introduced in 1959 – necessarily referred to in all publicity blurbs as the "New Sunbeam Alpine." Advertised as offering "sparkling performance... brilliantly teamed with style and comfort," the Alpine initially won American customers against stiff competition, partially because it had the small but significant comforts that so many British sports cars lacked. Tail fins, in line with American taste, were cunningly combined with exploitation of the Sunbeam name, which conferred the prestige of the authentic British sports car tradition. Of course, any connection with the prewar Sunbeam and its traditionally-crafted cars was strictly hokum, but the Alpine was nonetheless an attractively urbane two-seater.

Front view

Rear view

Side view

Auto option
From 1964, Sunbeam offered buyers automatic transmission.

Revised grille for the Series IV

Design and Production

Model	Sunbeam Alpine (1959–68)
Production	69,351
Body styles	Two-door roadster.
Construction	Unitary with X-bracing.
Engines	1494cc (MkI), 1592cc (MkII, III, IV), 1725cc (MkV).
Power output	83.5–99 bhp.
Transmission	Four-spped manual with optional overdrive.
Suspension	Front: independent; Rear: semi-elliptic with leaf springs.
Brakes	Front discs, rear drums.
Max speed	96 mph (155 km/h)

The styling of the Alpine, contracted out to Kenneth Howes, Geoff Crompton, and Roy Axe, was original and distinctive, but for the rest the car was very much a mix-and-match resorting of elements from other Rootes models. Maybe this makes it all stranger that it was not Rootes who initially built the Alpines. At the time that the car was entering development, the company was short of capacity at its Ryton-on-Dunsmore, England, factory, while Armstrong-Siddeley – on its last legs as a car manufacturer – had plenty of unused space at its Parkside factory in Coventry. A deal was struck for the Alpine to be developed and assembled by Armstrong-Siddeley, an arrangement that lasted from 1959 to the spring of 1962. Production of Alpines then shifted to Ryton, where they were turned out alongside the other Rootes models with which they shared so many parts in common. More than 69,000 Alpines were built from 1959 to 1968, during which time the car developed through five mostly marginally differentiated marks. Almost 12,000 of the MkI were made.

Reduced finnage
The fins were cut back for the Series IV models.

True racers
(right) Sunbeam had an established racing heritage, and when the Alpine was launched, publicity material played on the brand's rally successes. Alpines are still raced today, especially in classic and vintage race series in the US .

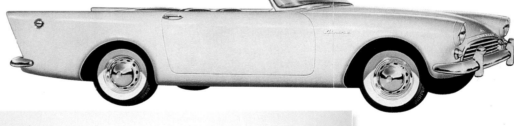

SLEEK · SWIFT · SPECTACULAR

THE NEW SUNBEAM ALPINE

Two's company
(above) The Alpine had a full-width seat behind the front seats, but it was only suitable for children or luggage. Even with a spare wheel, trunk space was ample.

Model choices
(left) The Series I came with a retractable top. Buyers could pay extra for the "sedan" feel and get a removable hardtop conversion.

The Sixties

"In the Sixties, America sucked up British sports cars like long lengths of spaghetti."

THE FLOWERING YEARS

1960

What a decade! Barely one year old and Jaguar fields its stunning E-Type *(see pages 124–27)*. A defining moment in the history of the sports car, the E offered everything to everyman. And all the fuss wasn't just because it was drop-dead pretty. The first of the 3.8s could hit 150 mph (242 km/h), carry a slick playboy and his baggage to Geneva and back in relative comfort, and cost only slightly more than a contemporary Jag sedan. No other machine before or since has so perfectly encapsulated the narcotic of the sports car: the E-Type made you look and feel like a movie star.

In the same year, Triumph rolled out its forgiving and well-mannered TR4; the MGB of '62 *(see pages 132–35)* was so civilized and uncomplicated that even a real estate agent could master it; and Mercedes' new pagoda roof 230SL felt as smooth and cosseting as a sedan. But sports cars weren't just becoming more refined, they were getting faster too. If you were determined enough the Austin Healey 3000 could hit 120 mph (193 km/h), as could the Sunbeam Tiger *(see pages 144–47)*, Daimler Dart *(see pages 112–15)*, and MGC. This was the sports car's halcyon age, when millions upon millions were spent developing, burnishing, and improving the breed. Rapid roadsters were selling like the elixir of youth.

Timeline 1960s

Lotus Seven

Porsche 356B

Daimler badge

1960
- John F. Kennedy is elected president of the US.
- A US experimental plane travels at almost 2,200 mph (3,542 km/h).
- Jaguar purchases rival car company Daimler.
- The first laser device is built and tested.
- In Britain, Prince Andrew is born. He is the first child born to a reigning monarch since 1857.

1961
- Yuri Gagarin, the Soviet cosmonaut, is the first man in space. He orbits the earth several times before returning safely.
- The Triumph TR4 is launched to the public.
- The Berlin Wall is built.
- Cuban rebels armed by the US attempt an unsuccessful invasion of Cuba at the Bay of Pigs.

1962
- The Cuban missile crisis occurs, with the USSR and the US close to nuclear war.
- The first children affected by the anti-morning sickness drug thalidomide are born.
- The MGB and legendary AC Cobra are launched.

1963
- President John F. Kennedy is shot and assassinated in Dallas, Texas.
- The Alfa Romeo Spider is replaced by the Giulia series.
- Russian Valentina Tereshkova becomes the first female astronaut. She is in space for three days.

1964
- A US ship is destroyed off North Vietnam and North Vietnamese bases are bombed by the US in retaliatory attacks.
- Porsche introduce the 356C with disc brakes.
- The "Brain Drain" starts, with British scientists moving to the US in increasing numbers.
- Ian Fleming, author of the James Bond books, dies.
- Cassius Clay wins the world heavyweight boxing championship.

INCREASED PERFORMANCE

Ordinary owners could now choose from a traffic jam of extremely speedy machines. The AC Cobra *(see pages 148–51)*, Ferrari Daytona, Maserati Ghibli, and Porsche 911 *(see pages 200–03)* offered epic performance and are still considered fast today. Bodies got stiffer, handling more precise, and steering crisper. Tire technology improved, suspension settings became a black art, and companies like Ferrodo and Lockheed made brakes that stopped like never before. By the end of the decade many Sixties sports and GT cars had the sort of finishing-school road manners that could only be dreamed of 10 years earlier.

And they got cheaper too. Entry to the smart convertible set often cost only marginally more than ordinary four-door fare. Cars like the Triumph Spitfire *(see pages 128–31,* and MG Midget were budget blasters, which despite prosaic sedan mechanicals could still cut a dash in suburbia. But most important of all, the sports car had become both reliable and easy to own. The era of the second car had dawned and the middle classes bought two-seaters for the little lady or just a little weekend fun. Every carmaker had at least one in its model lineup, and every hairdresser at least two parked outside. The sports car was now the darling of the smart set.

- Protests are held by US students against the Vietnam War.

- The British Grand Prix starts to alternate between the Brands Hatch and Silverstone race circuits.

- The Aston Martin DB6 is launched.

- The General Post Office Tower is opened in London.

- Jim Clark becomes world car racing champion.

- Winston Churchill dies.

Jaguar E-Type

- The Jensen Interceptor FF is introduced.

- In the Vietnam War, a 48-hour truce is observed over Christmas.

- Floods in Italy destroy thousands of art treasures in Florence.

- Miniskirts come into fashion.

- US spacecraft *Surveyor I* lands on the moon.

- The Six-Day War between Israel and the Arab nations takes place.

- Dr. Christiann Barnard carries out the first human heart transplant in Cape Town, South Africa.

- British model Twiggy becomes famous in the US.

- The first Pontiac Firebirds are produced.

- The People's Republic of China detonates its first hydrogen bomb.

- Three US astronauts are killed in a fire on the launching pad, leading to the suspension of US manned space flights.

Carroll Shelby

- Ferrari launches the world's fastest car – the Daytona 365 GTB/4 V12.

- Reverend Martin Luther King Jr. is assassinated in a Memphis motel room.

- Czechoslovakia is invaded by Soviet troops.

- The Aswan Dam is built.

Ad for the MGB

- Datsun enters the US sports market with its 240Z.

- Neil Armstrong steps out of Apollo 11 to become the first man to walk on the moon.

- British troops are sent into Northern Ireland.

1965 **1966** **1967** **1968** **1969**

LOTUS SEVEN

Colin Chapman knew that enthusiasts were Lotus's lifeblood and that selling Elites to the middle classes wouldn't keep the bank happy for long. So in 1957, he launched a cheap sports car for what he called "the woolly hat brigade." In a brilliant ruse, he sold the car in kit-form, thereby bypassing British tax laws. Not only would car buffs enjoy all that tinkering at home, but the price would undercut the competition by a mile. And so the Lotus Seven was born.

The nearest thing to a four-wheeled motorcycle, the Seven was quick, handled like a go-kart, and was exceptional fun. Nobody cared that it was as comfortable as a cave, rode as smoothly as a tram, and had a top that was as easy to put up as a tent; the Seven went like the wind. Various attempts at civilizing the model followed, and in 1970, Lotus capitalized on the buggy craze with a curvy new body for the Series IV, which bombed. Chapman sold the rights to the Seven to Caterham Cars in 1973, who continue to make the Caterham Seven to this day.

Wide power choice
From the first 1957 Series I to the sale of the Seven to Caterham Cars in '73, the Seven was offered with eight different engine options.

Series I

Series IV

Caterham Seven

Keeping it real
With Lotus literature describing
it as "the ideal choice for the
man who would like to build
his own car," the Seven was
strictly for those who saw the
car as a project instead of a
fashion statement.

The magnificent Seven – grassroots racer

Lotus publicity material described the self-assemble Seven as "principally intended for the milder forms of competition motoring". But there was nothing mild about the driving experience a Seven afforded. With its free-standing headlights and tacked-on front fenders it owed nothing to the science of aerodynamics; but this hardly mattered since it was so light and highly powered for its weight. In hill climbs and sprints the Seven was hard to beat. This car had no hint of comfort. There were no doors, only cutaway sides, and if you did manage to put the top up – no mean feat – you would find it was almost impossible to climb in and out of the car. Self-assembly carried no quality guarantees, and many enthusiasts put together Sevens that were downright dangerous. But ultimately few cars can ever have been so loved by their owners.

Front view

Rear view

Side view

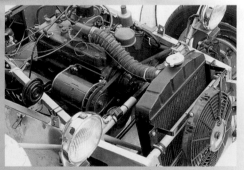

Engine
The Series I came with an 1172cc Ford block as standard. In addition to a souped-up version of this unit there was also the option of an 1098cc Coventry Climax engine. Later Sevens came with beefier Ford blocks and a Lotus Twin Cam unit.

"All early Sevens left the factory with unpainted aluminum bodywork for buyers to paint in their chosen color."

Steering wheel
The wood-rim steering wheel was standard on Super models.

Folded-down windshield

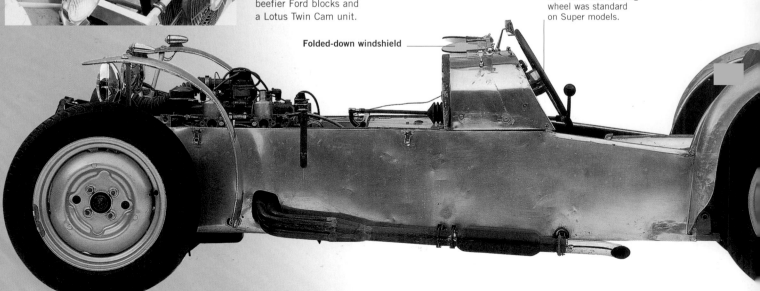

Design and Production

Model	Lotus Seven (1957–73)
Production	2,813 (S1–S4)
Body style	Two-seat convertible.
Construction	Tubular chassis with alloy/steel/GRP body.
Engines	948cc, 1098cc, 1172cc, 1340cc, 1498cc, 1558cc, 1598cc four-cylinder.
Power output	40–120 bhp
Transmission	Three- and four-speed manual
Suspension	Front: independent with coil springs; Rear: independent with coil springs.
Brakes	Drums all around; later front discs, rear drums.
Max speed	76–116 mph (122–187 km/h)

The heart of the Lotus Seven "kit" delivered to its purchaser was a well-designed multitubular space frame chassis and an aluminum body. The cars had coil-sprung independent front suspension and a live rear axle. Over the years these features were married with a range of engines and transmissions. Initially the side-valve Ford 100E unit with three-speed gearbox was standard, but the Seven was later available with other variants of Ford engines or the BMC unit from the Sprite *(see pages 92–95)*. At the extreme, Lotus Ford powerplants were used, generating around 120 bhp. The rough and risky Seven fit poorly with the sleek Lotus image by the late 1960s, and Colin Chapman was no doubt glad enough to find a convenient pretext for selling off the rights when the introduction of sales tax in 1973 ended the tax-exemption that had been fundamental to the economy of the self-assembly market.

Mini windshield
(left) A full-width windshield came as standard, but these small, individual Plexiglas screens could be ordered as an extra. Quick-release latches allowed removal of the dash and cowl for easy access to the rear of the instrument panel and front suspension.

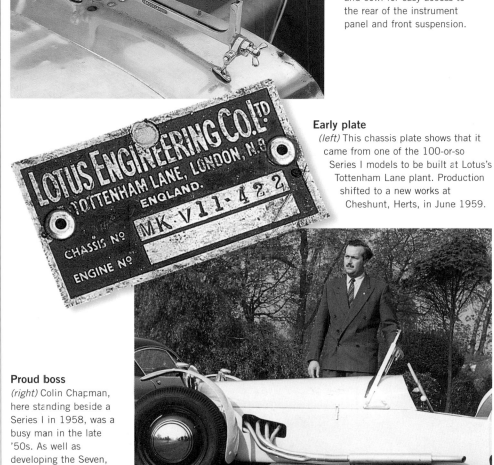

Early plate
(left) This chassis plate shows that it came from one of the 100-or-so Series I models to be built at Lotus's Tottenham Lane plant. Production shifted to a new works at Cheshunt, Herts, in June 1959.

Interior
(above) The red interior was matched by a PVC-covered dash within which were set a 0–100 mph (161 km/h) speedometer, oil pressure gauge, water temperature gauge, and ammeter. A fuel gauge wasn't introduced until the Series III of 1968.

Proud boss
(right) Colin Chapman, here standing beside a Series I in 1958, was a busy man in the late '50s. As well as developing the Seven, he simultaneously released the first of his road cars, the Elite.

CUX·C 7

In the blood
Porsche's association with motorsport
is almost as old as the brand itself. In
1951 the second 356 prototype won
the 1100cc category at Le Mans.

Man of taste
(far right) Steve McQueen's
penchant for the beautiful things
in life extended beyond the female
form to cars such as the 356.

Porsche aficionado
(right) James Dean's need for
speed influenced his ultimately,
fatal decision to trade in his 356
Speedster for a 505 Spyder.

**"One look at the timeless shape of the later
Porsche 911 shows you just how right
the 356's original design was."**

PORSCHE 356B

When Ferry Porsche first conceived the 356 in 1948, Germany was in the postwar doldrums, restricted by economic sanctions, and desperate to get itself back on track. The Porsche company had relocated to Austria and Ferry enlisted the services of an Austrian, Irwin Kommeda, to design the 356's bodywork. The first 356s were produced in 1950, and over the next 16 years a series of increasingly advanced models were rolled out.

With the 356A of 1956 came a 1600cc engine upgrade, and by this time the car was causing a stir in the US. The '59 356B continued the trend of offering advanced specifications for Porsche owners. Finned aluminum brake drums and improved syncromesh on the gearbox were impressive, but not as significant as the new Super 90 unit. By 1964, production for the year exceeded that for the previous 10 years combined and coincided with the birth of the 911. The 356, then, went out on a high, and ushered in an era where buyers began to worship at the high altar of German engineering efficiency.

The classic 356 – birth of the Porsche profile

Ferry Porsche's 356 was originally based on his father Ferdinand's famous prewar design, the Volkswagen. With its air-cooled, flat-four rear engine, trailing-link front suspension, and swing-axle rear suspension, the 356 was essentially a hot VW with aerodynamic bodywork. Over the years, a variety of models and engine upgrades took the car progressively further from its origins, and by the time the 356B appeared in 1959 there were had hardly any VW parts left. Still, the distinctive layout remained, making the 356 unlike any other sports model. Racing success helped to sell the cars, with a notable class win at Le Mans in 1951. The alloy-bodied Carrera version, with disc-brakes and a twin-cam 1600cc engine, was produced specifically with competition in mind – it could reach 124 mph (200 km/h). Even basic production models could achieve 100 mph (161 km/h).

Front view

Rear view

Side view

Design and Production

Model	Porsche 356B (1959–63)
Production	30,963
Body styles	Two-plus-two fixed-head coupe, convertible, and Speedster.
Construction	Unitary steel body with integral pressed-steel platform chassis.
Engine	Air-cooled, horizontally opposed flat four 1582cc with twin carbs.
Power output	90 bhp at 5500 rpm (Super 90).
Transmission	Four-speed manual, all synchromesh, rear-wheel drive.
Suspension	Front: independent, trailing arms with transverse torsion bars and anti-roll bar; Rear: independent, swing half-axles, radius arms, and transverse torsion bars. Telescopic shocks.
Brakes	Hydraulic drums all around.
Max speed	110 mph (177 km/h)

The first Porsche 356s were hand-built at Gmünd, Austria, and had alloy bodywork. But shortages of components and skilled labor in Austria, among other factors, meant that production was quickly switched to Stuttgart-Zufenhausen in West Germany. There the 356 was put into series production, with steel bodies replacing alloy. The 356 was the first car with the Porsche logo. Although Ferdinand Porsche died in 1951, his prestigious name undoubtedly helped the car to sell. Its price, modest for a vehicle with such looks and performance, was another selling point. Design was successfully updated from time to time, the 356A, for example, bringing in a one-piece windshield, and the 356B seeing the introduction of bumpers. The 356 had a quiet and relatively economical engine, and won an enviable reputation for reliability and durability over its 16 years in production. In total 76,305 were built.

Early sketches
(right) These technical drawings, possibly dating from 1947, illustrate the 356 prototype. The production model didn't change too much from the original concept, with the prototype's awesome handling and speed being maintained. Model 356-001 – the first working prototype – currently resides at Porsche's factory museum.

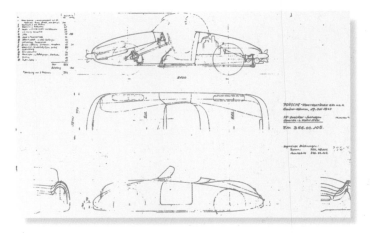

Father of the Porsche
(left) Ferdinand Porsche conceived the VW Beetle and used profits made from the "people's car" to set up the Porsche brand after World War II. It was his son, Ferry, who played a greater role in the 356, often testing the prototype himself.

Engine
(above) The original 356 had an 1100cc block mounted onto the rear of the car, with a 1300 unit available in 1951, a 1500 Super released in '52, and a 1600 – as seen on this 356B – in '55. The last 356s were equipped with 1996cc blocks.

Interior
(left) The 356's interior was elegantly functional, with four green-on-black dials set on a brushed aluminium, padded dash. The gear lever may have been long by sports standards, but Porsche's patented baulk-ring synchromesh ensured smooth changes.

Gelatin mold
(right) Original 1949 356s such as this were more bulbous and had lower bumpers than the B. And the split windshield was genuine compared to the deceptive chrome rearview mirror bar on later convertible models.

Big-block express
Straight-line speed was never a problem for the Dart, especially with a 2.5-liter V8 under the hood. It was, at the time, Britain's only V8 aside from Rolls' Silver Cloud II block.

Daimler
PRESENTS THE V8 S.P. 250

Empty promises
Daimler copywriters promised "impeccable cornering" and featherl ght handling," but in reality, the Dart had such poor roadholding that the chassis had to be stiffened in 1961.

DAIMLER
SP250 DART

People usually equate Daimler with stately executive cruisers, but there was a time when the company ventured into producing other styles – the SP250 Dart was the sportiest model Daimler ever made. Born out of a financial crisis at Daimler in the late 1950s, a committee was set up in 1958 to look at the possibility of Daimler producing a sports model; as well as Daimler chiefs, there were also top guns from BSA and Triumph present. When released at the 1959 New York Show, the Dart's unusual amalgam of European and American styling themes indicated that it had been designed with an eye on the American market. But the buying public were unsure about the glass-reinforced-plastic body built on top of the standard girder chassis. And they weren't convinced by Daimler's pricing policy, which meant that usually standard components and body parts such as the heater and bumpers were classed as optional extras.

Jaguar took over Daimler in 1960 and monitored progress of the Dart, but poor sales, especially in the US, meant that Sir William Lyons pulled the plug four years later. No real surprise, considering that the original sales projection of 7,500 units in the first three years fell short by a crippling 4,800 cars. A quirky entry into the classic sports car hall of fame, then, and not without its positive points – the engine, for example, was as smooth as silk – but the Dart was a brave, if ill-conceived, attempt to cash in on the reputation of the British sports car. Ultimately, it was the car that finished Daimler.

Daimler's sporty Dart – poorly-executed design

The key figure behind the Daimler SP250 was Edward Turner, who had made his name as a designer of Triumph motorbike engines. Newly installed as Daimler's managing director, Turner was able to create an engine that presented the company with a way into the potentially lucrative North American sports car market. A 2548cc V8 generating 140 bhp, it gave the SP250 acceleration from 0–60 (96 km/h) in 10 seconds and a top speed of 125 mph (201 km/h). Although praise for the engine was almost universal, customers were generally underwhelmed by the styling of the car's fiberglass body, which was certainly too elaborate to satisfy sports car purists. Marketing of the SP250 in the US also suffered an early setback when the chosen name "Dart" had to be dropped because of a copyright dispute with Dodge.

Front view

Rear view

Side view

Interior
The classic British interior was all leather seats and thick-pile carpets. The wind-up windows helped to keep the occupants unruffled when the V8 kicked in.

Fiberglass body

VVS 343

Design and Production

Model	Daimler SP250 Dart (1959–64)
Production	2,644 (1,415 lhd, 1229 rhd)
Body style	Two-door, two-seater sports convertible.
Construction	Fiberglass body, steel girder chassis.
Engine	Iron-block 2548cc V8.
Power output	140 bhp at 5800 rpm.
Transmission	Four-speed manual or three-speed Borg-Warner Model 8.
Suspension	Front: independent with wishbones and coil springs; Rear: live axle with leaf springs.
Brakes	Four-wheel Girling discs.
Max speed	125 mph (201 km/h)

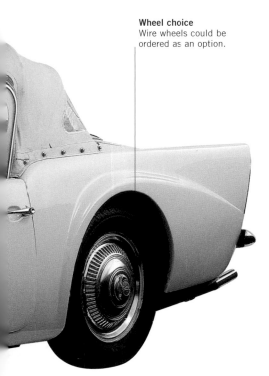

Wheel choice
Wire wheels could be ordered as an option.

With no previous experience in the sports car area, and a financial situation that left no room for mistakes, Daimler sensibly copied the chassis, suspension, and transmission of the SP250 from a successful rival, the Triumph TR3A (although this meant their car inherited the Triumph's hard, basic ride). To these elements, Daimler added Turner's superb 2548cc V8 engine. Daimler was able to build its own engines and transmissions, and had the chassis made by a component supplier. But the expense of tooling up to make the body threatened to be prohibitive – therefore the decision to use fiberglass for the body instead of steel. There were some complaints about lack of stiffness and poor finish in the Dart's body, although these were largely teething troubles. Though very few SP250s were built, the engine lived on as the powerplant of the Daimler V8-250 sedan.

Pursuit vehicle
(right) With an ad line of "Built to go places... fast!" the Dart was the perfect model for law enforcement; the British Metropolitan Police bought a fleet of 30.

Transatlantic influence
(left) With Harley Earl, Cadillac's chief stylist, working the fin theme in the US, it was no surprise that the trend would spread to British manufacturers.

BUILT TO GO PLACES... *FAST!*

Daimler V8 S.P. 250

Making the Dart
(left) Daimler's idea of manufacturing a sports model was flawed in a number of ways, one of which was that the design was rushed through, resulting in a painfully slow production line. Jaguar, for example, produced and sold 22,000 cars in 1959; Daimler could only manage a few hundred Darts. Total production over the five years was a measly 2,644 cars.

AUSTIN HEALEY
3000

Though officially released in 1959, the Austin-Healey 3000's origins go back a few years earlier. After scoring a hit with the Healey 100 at the 1952 Earl's Court Show in London, Austin's chief, Leonard Lord, made a deal with Donald Healey to build the complete car instead of just supplying its engines as had been the case previously. The new model was immediately rebranded the Austin-Healey 100 and given a more than reasonable $1,000 (£750) price tag. Healey's hunch that there was a gap in the American market between the MG T series *(see pages 24–27)* and the Jaguar XK120 *(see pages 28–31)* was proved right; over 80 percent of cars went to the US.

Through the Fifties, the 100 received stylistic accolades, notched up many notable racing victories, and became an incredible export success – less than four per cent of the cars stayed in the UK. A new six-cylinder unit replaced the four in 1956 (Austin-Healey 100-6), and the 3000 plate arrived three years later. The rebranded model came with a rebored 2912cc six, which boosted power output to 124 bhp, and by the time the Mark III ceased production in 1968, the 3000 was capable of an impressive 195 km/h (121 mph) from its 148 bhp engine. During the 3000's nine-year lifespan, additions such as front disc brakes, wind-up windows, and a wraparound windshield turned it into a refined sports cruiser. The model also helped to secure Austin-Healey's reputation as a maker of thoroughbred classic sports cars.

Fifty years strong
The Austin-Healey marque celebrated its Golden Anniversary in 2002. Thousands of owners of the "Big Healeys," such as the 3000, and the smaller Sprite *(see pages 92–95)* can tell you how well their cars have stood the test of time.

"There are few finer examples of a surefooted, thoroughbred sports car than the Austin-Healey 3000"

Screen star
The Austin-Healey 100 and the later 3000 were glamorous enough to star in a number of movies. Here, an example features in the 1957 movie *April Love*.

The handsome Healey – quintessentially British

The Healey's success was due to one important virtue – it looked so masculine. The stance was agressive, the lines muscular, and that long hood promised performance. Ads and brochures showed tweedy women driving Healeys, but in truth, the 3000 was a hard car to drive well, though one that richly rewarded press-on-progress. Hot, cramped, and very tail happy, you needed complete concentration and the reactions of a fighter pilot to drive it seriously fast. The definitive British Bulldog, the 3000 was a man's car for a man's world. Girls in Britain drove Sunbeam Alpines, real estate agents drove MGBs and ladies' men chose the caddish Jaguar XK150, but real men, usually with the biceps to prove it, drove Austin-Healey 3000s. Even the E-Type was considered too soft and self-conscious in comparison. No other sports car, before or since, has offered that brutish Healey appeal.

Front view

Rear view

Side view

Limited storage space

Hot spot
The cockpit was invariably a hot place to be, due to its close proximity to the engine and exhaust.

Wraparound windshield
from 1962

Design and Production

Model	Austin-Healey 3000 (1959–68)
Production	42,926 (all 3000 models)
Body styles	Two-seater roadster, 2+2 roadster, 2+2 convertible.
Construction	Separate chassis/body.
Engine	2912cc overhead-valve, straight-six.
Power output	Mk I: 124 bhp at 4600 rpm; Mk II: 132 bhp at 4750 rpm; Mk III: 150 bhp at 5250 rpm.
Transmission	Four-speed manual with overdrive.
Suspension	Front: independent coil springs and wishbones, antiroll bar; Rear: semi-elliptic leaf springs. Lever-arm shocks all around.
Brakes	Front discs; rear drum.
Max speed	110–121 mph (177–195 km/h)

Like many great cars, the Big Healey took a while before it hit the big time. The original 100/4 was too slow, and the more powerful 100/6 was too heavy. Dealers, customers, and even the Healey family repeatedly urged BMC to make the Austin-Healey go as well as it looked. Things only started to happen in '57 with a new six-port cylinder head, which upped the power to a respectable 117 bhp. But the big change came in '59 with the new 2912cc engine. Along with that glorious noise, power went up to 124 bhp, giving a brisk maximum speed of 120 mph (193 km/h). Front disc brakes helped to keep the speed in check and the steering was tickled to make it even crisper. The result was one of the most successful cars ever to pass through the famous Abingdon-based competitions department, and one that was to dominate every rally event for the next six years.

Attracting the well-heeled
(left) Austin-Healey used advertising to attract wealthy buyers to the 3000, even though it was cheaper than most of its sporting contemporaries. Using a racehorse in the image couldn't fail to suggest a link between the car and good breeding.

Race legends
(right) Paddy Hopkirk and navigator alongside their 1965 factory 3000. A 3000 driven by Timo Makinen came second in the Rally of Great Britain that year.

Brochure
(below) The 3000's sales brochure emphasized the model's engine. The Mk III could hit 100 (161 km/h) in 25.7 seconds.

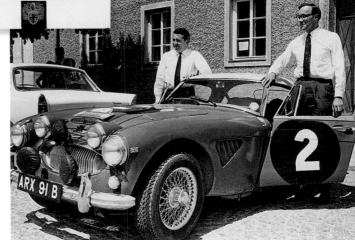

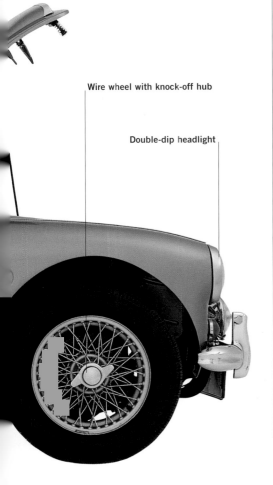

Wire wheel with knock-off hub

Double-dip headlight

FACEL VEGA
FACELLIA

The Facellia was meant to open up the prestigious Facel brand to a wider audience. Facel's autocratic creator, Jean Daninos, wanted his new car to have an entirely new engine. So rather than use another car company's block, as he'd done previously, he approached Pont-a-Mousson, who already built Facel gearboxes. On paper the new four-cylinder unit looked good, with twin overhead cams and 115 bhp.

Within weeks of the Facellia's launch, owners were reporting misfires, oil leaks, and eventual piston failure. Facel bled to death honoring warranty claims; two years were wasted trying to identify a cooling problem; and even using Volvo 1800 and Healey units couldn't reverse the car's ailing fortunes. Word was out: France's new sports car was a dog. Which was a shame, because the pretty Facellia should have sold quicker than croissants.

French flair
(below) Oozing Gallic class, Facels were *the* cars to be seen in during the late Fifties.

Deceptive dash
(below right) Though the dashboard looked like walnut, it was actually painted metal.

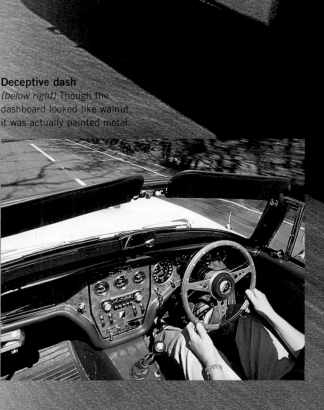

A great reputation
In terms of finish and quality, Facels were looked upon in the highest regard, known for their attention to detail and great engineering. Until, that is, the Facellia.

The unfortunate Facellia – a mechanical letdown

Jean Daninos's Facel engineering company had made everything from car bodies to jet engine parts and office furniture before turning to the manufacture of its own luxury cars in 1954. The Facel Vegas at first looked as if they might be a considerable success, and a decision to build a smaller two-seat sports version of the Vega was made in 1957. The Facellia's look was a straightforward scaled-down version of larger Facel models such as the HK 500, and was similarly handsome. The interior of the car was also superbly decked out and the handling was good. Unfortunately, the decision to have the engine custom-built by Facel's gearbox manufacturer Pont-a-Mousson proved fatal. It could not be made to work reliably until two years after the Facellia's launch in 1959, by which time the Facel company was on a slippery downward slope.

Front view

Rear view

Side view

Bodywork
The pressed-steel bodyshell was welded to the chassis.

"Without its engine problems, the Facellia would have been a great car."

First block
Twin-overhead cam engine.

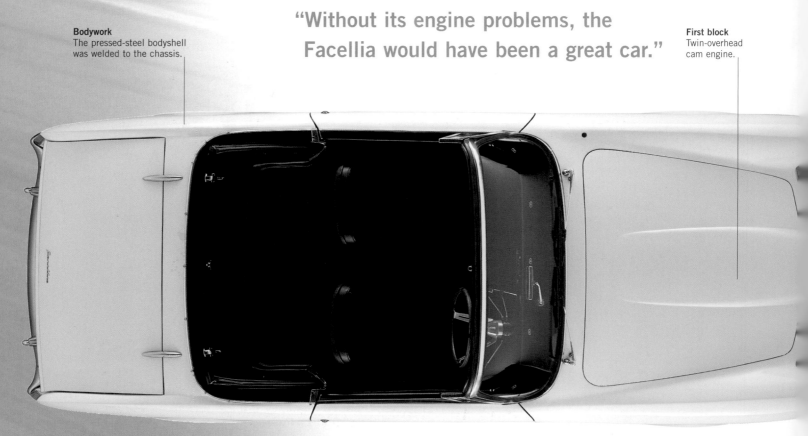

Design and Production

Model	Facel Vega Facellia (1960–64)
Production	1,767 (small-engined Facels)
Body style	Two-seat convertible.
Construction	Steel body and chassis.
Engine	1647cc four-cylinder.
Power output	115 bhp.
Transmission	Four-speed manual.
Suspension	Front: independent with coil springs; Rear: semi-elliptic leaf springs.
Brakes	Discs all around.
Max speed	106 mph (171 km/h)

Facel believed it was well-placed to produce its own cars, having lots of experience making bodywork for the likes of Simca and Panhard. The Facellia had a pressed-steel body welded onto a tubular chassis at the company's Colombes factory. The engine was designed by Carlo Marchetti, who had previously done respectable work for Talbot. It was a unit of thoroughly modern conception, a 1.6-liter engine with twin-overhead camshaft and an output of 115 bhp. Its tendency to burn pistons and leak oil was correctable, but only given time, which Facel did not have. The Facellia was relaunched in 1963 as the Facel III, with a dull but reliable Volvo 1.8-liter P1800 engine, and in 1964 a few Facel 6s appeared, the same car again but this time with a version of the Austin-Healey 3000 powerplant. Probably around 500 Facellias were built, about 1,500 Facel IIIs, and a handful of Facel 6s.

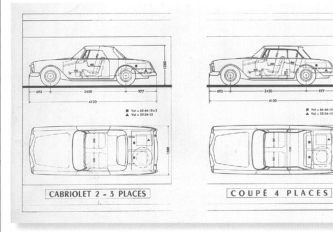

CABRIOLET 2 - 3 PLACES

COUPÉ 4 PLACES

Model choice
(left) The Facellia came in convertible or coupe forms, with Facel claiming the soft top could fit one extra body in the back and the hardtop two. Despite an overall length of 13½ ft (4.1 m), the Facellia was still smaller than previous Facels.

Interior
The simple dashboard consisted of a speedometer and tachometer, with smaller dials and various switchgear positioned on the left. A medium-long wave radio with automatic antenna was optional. The steering wheel was large, as was the Facellia's turning circle of 32 ft (9.7 m).

Air of sophistication
(right) Facel had always presented itself as a classy European brand, attracting buyers from Britain and the US who wanted to own an exclusive set of European wheels. And while its Vega model had established a good reputation for the company, the problems associated with the Facellia undid all the previous good work.

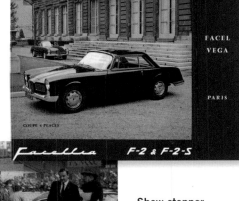

FACEL VEGA PARIS

Facellia F-2 & F-2-S

Show stopper
(left) When displayed at the 1959 Paris Salon, the Facellia was well received. The public liked Facel's mix of European styling and American horsepower on the larger models and were equally impressed by the 100 percent French smaller model.

JAGUAR E-TYPE

On March 15, 1961, Jaguar did what it had done before with its XK120 *(see pages 28–31)* – took the public's breath away with the unveiling of a new model. This time the location was the Geneva Motor Show, and the car was the E-Type. And while the XK120 had been an undoubted success, it was nothing compared to the critical acclaim given to Jaguar's new baby, not to mention the astounding production figures that followed over the E-Type's 13-year production run.

As for the secrets of the E-Type's success, well, there were none. One look at that awesome hood and pert tail told you it was an automotive masterpiece of truly classic proportions. Getting behind the wheel and driving the E-Type – or XKE as it's sometimes known in the US – created another level of excitement again as the original 3781cc straight-six purred its way to over 140 mph (225 km/h) on an advanced independent rear suspension system. This time Jaguar had really excelled itself with its usual combination of looks, performance, and value for money – no wonder the E-Type was a milestone in the history of the British sports car.

Top Cat
(right) Superb aerodynamic styling, a range of sweet, powerful engines, and legendary Jaguar performance have made the E-Type one of *the* ultimate sports cars.

Low-slung beast
(below) During its lifespan, the E-Type had a number of engine upgrades, chassis modifications, and body restyles. The one constant was ground clearance, which remained a roadhugging 5 in (8 cm) throughout.

1963 Series I 3.8 Fixed Head Coupe   1965 Series I 4.2 Fixed Head Coupe   1966 Series I 4.2 2+2 Fixed Head Coupe

CAT·186
NSW — THE PREMIER STATE

1972 Series III V12 Roadster   1972 Series III V12 Fixed Head Coupe

The sublime E-Type – top of the Cats

Originally conceived in 1956–57 as
a racing successor to the D-Type, the
E-Type represented the triumph of
an uncompromising attitude to design.
Aerodynamicist Malcolm Sayer was given
free reign to create the most streamlined
shape that lengthy experiments in a wind
tunnel could deliver. Under the hood was
the 13-year-old 3.8-liter XK six-cylinder
engine, replaced in 1964 by a 4.2-liter
version. Initially, Jaguar's problem with
the E-Type was not selling the cars, but
producing enough to satisfy demand. With
astonishing looks and a claimed maximum
speed of 150 mph (241 km/h), the E had
celebrities queuing up to buy. Although a
bit cramped, the car was pure luxury to
drive, combining genuine sports car
performance with a smooth ride and
excellent roadholding. And all for under
$5,900 (£2,100) for the '61 roadster.

Front view

Rear view

Side view

Block head
Straight-six cylinder
configuration.

Wishbone suspension

Design and Production

Model	Jaguar E-Type (1961–74)
Production	72,520
Body styles	Two-seater roadster and fixed coupé, 2+2 fixed head coupe.
Construction	Steel monocoque
Engines	3781cc straight-six, 4235cc straight-six, 5343cc V12.
Power output	265 to 272 bhp.
Transmission	Four-speed manual, optional automatic in 1966.
Suspension	Front: independent, wishbones and torsion bar; Rear: independent, coil and radius arm.
Brakes	Discs all around.
Max speed	150 mph (241 km/h) (3.8 and 4.2); 143 mph (230 km/h) (5.3 V12)

Jaguar adopted a monocoque steel body and chassis for the E-Type, even though this was expensive and difficult to manufacture. The body/chassis was bolted to a tubular pressed-steel front frame, with coil-sprung independent rear suspension. The car was available in two versions: an open-top roadster and a fastback coupé, both two-seaters. The upgrade of the engine from 3.8 to 4.2 liters in 1964 was accompanied by the introduction of an all-syncromesh transmission. In 1966, the two-seater models were joined by a 2+2 coupe version, with a longer wheelbase providing for the extra seating, and an automatic option. By the late 1960s, performance of production E-Types was declining as Jaguar struggled to adapt the car to new US environmental and safety legislation. Over 57,000 six-cylinder E-types were built up to 1971 (almost 11,000 of them 2+2s), after which the V12 model continued for a few extra years.

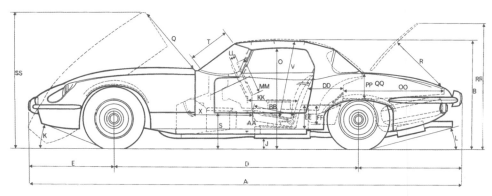

Work it out
(above) Designer Malcolm Sayer claimed that the E-Type was the first car to be "mathematically designed." The original model's wheelbase was lengthened by 9 in (23 cm) on the 1966 2+2 and later V12.

New facility
(right) Jaguar's purchase of Daimler in 1960 allowed it to use the integrated company's larger plant in Coventry, England, for car assembly.

Restricted access
It was a case of watching your head on the semi-opening hood.

Dunlop SP41 HR tire

Breathers
All UK models were equipped with triple SU carburetors.

Peak output
(left) For every three E-Types built, two were exported, and with foreign buyers eagerly snapping up the model it made for a busy time on the production lines. By 1966, the total value of Jaguar's postwar exports amounted to $300 (£200) million.

Handle with care
The Spitfire gave thousands of drivers years of driving pleasure, though even the Mk3's handling could be described as a little testing.

Rooftop problems
Early models like this preMk3 offered the convertible experience, but at a price; the top was a complicated affair that took forever to put together and disassemble.

TRIUMPH
SPITFIRE MK3

Never a great car, but always a pretty one, the Spitfire did good business for Triumph. The Coventry, England, firm's first small sports car, Spitfires racked up an impressive production total of 314,342 units in 18 years. Gievanni Michelotti's neat styling was the main attraction, along with a spacious cabin, eager performance, and that astonishing turning circle of just 24 ft (7.3 m). Nobody cared that the mechanicals were mundane, or that the rear end was decidedly twitchy in the wet, Triumph's little fighter had a classy carelessness and was leagues more refined than the contemporary Sprites *(see pages 92–95)* and Midgets with which it was in competition.

And if you opted for wire wheels, a snug hardtop, and overdrive, you owned a practical, stylish two-seater that was amazingly economical. The gear change was slick and the exhaust note sporty, even though it couldn't quite touch the magic "ton." The MkI had a hood you raised like a tent and only 63 bhp. More power came with the Mk2, but at just 4 bhp extra it was nothing to get too excited about. Serious improvements to the car came with the Mk3 in '67, when Triumph gave the Spit a foldaway hood, 75 bhp, and wider wheels. 1971 saw a body restyle and handling improvements, but in 1974 an emission-strangled American spec 1500 engine was put into all Spits. By then, quality control had nose-dived and the last car rolled out of the Solihull, England, factory in the summer of 1980.

The spirited Spitfire – Triumph's pocket best-seller

To sell a car like the Spitfire, you had to make sure nobody noticed that a large part of what they were buying consisted of parts of a mundane sedan – in the Spitfire's case including a very shady swing-axle rear suspension. Pulling power and a slice of British tradition were the twin attractions highlighted in one Spitfire advertising slogan: "You not only get a car and a girl but a piece of history." The history was the entirely fictional connection with the famous Battle of Britain fighter. Success in competition helped underline the fact that the car was no mean performer – for instance, Spitfires were first and second in class at Le Mans in 1965 and had a string of successes in rallies, where the celebrated 24-ft (7.3-m) turning circle came in handy. Above all it looked the part and the styling lasted remarkably well over the series' long production life.

Front view

Rear view

Side view

Engine
The Mk3 Spitfire's 1296cc block was 12 percent more powerful than the Mk2's unit.

"Though more expensive than its Sprite competitor, the Spitfire was a far better seller."

Full-length hood

Design and Production

Model	Triumph Spitfire (1962–80)
Production	314,332
Body style	Two-seat sports convertible with optional steel hardtop.
Construction	Steel body and chassis.
Engines	1147cc, 1296cc, 1493cc four-cylinder.
Power output	63–71 bhp.
Transmission	Four-speed manual with optional overdrive.
Suspension	Front: independent with coil spring; Rear: transverse leaf spring.
Brakes	Front disc, rear drums.
Max speed	90-95 mph (145–153 km/h)

It was apparently on his own initiative that Italian designer Giovanni Michelotti decided to style a two-seat sports version of the Triumph Herald sedan. When Triumph bosses saw the result, they wisely decided to pick it up and run with it. The Spitfire emerged in 1962 with a Herald four-cylinder engine, transmission, and suspension, but an entirely original backbone channeled-steel girder chassis. The steel-panel bodywork was also all-new, with a single combined hood and fender section allowing the whole front of the car to open up for inspection of the engine. Spitfires of different types rolled off the production lines at Triumph's Coventry factory for 18 years. The Mark 3 of 1967 was one of the best received models, with its engine having grown from the original 1147cc to 1296cc, generating 75 bhp and somewhat optimistically claimed to give a maximum speed of 100 mph (161 km/h).

Similar dimensions
(left) There was not much to differentiate between the Mk3 and previous models on the size front. The contoured bucket seats were, though, an improvement.

Tricky tail end
(below) Publicity for the Mk3 talked of its great roadholding on the steel girder chassis, but the swing axle rear suspension meant cornering was not particularly surefooted.

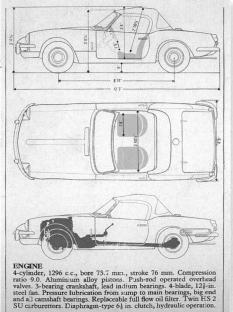

ENGINE
4-cylinder, 1296 c.c., bore 73.7 mm., stroke 76 mm. Compression ratio 9.0. Aluminium alloy pistons. Push-rod operated overhead valves. 3-bearing crankshaft, lead indium bearings. 4-blade, 12¼-in. steel fan. Pressure lubrication from sump to main bearings, big end and all camshaft bearings. Replaceable full flow oil filter. Twin HS 2 SU carburettors. Diaphragm-type 6¼ in. clutch, hydraulic operation.

Lockable trunk

Block pride
(right) Triumph's Mk3 brochure led with this image of a bored woman waiting while the men finished getting their satisfaction from under the hood. And it was a pretty fair reflection of the situation, as the model's big news was the improved engine. Copy talked of "fuss-free" performance and "effortless power" and many track racers found this to be true.

**Triumph introduce the new Spitfire Mark 3
The big news is under the bonnet!**

MGB

The MGB took the baton from the MGA *(see pages 76–79)* in 1962 and ran with it. The world's best-selling single model sports car – over half a million were produced – was a perfect mix of reliability, practicality, and good sense, with timeless good looks and brisk performance thrown in for good measure. Using essentially the same transmission, suspension, and engine as the A, the B's major difference – aside from a few design alterations – was that it incorporated the unitary construction that was all the rage in the early 1960s. It was also shorter than the previous model, though MG's design team was able to create a bigger cockpit for the B.

1965 saw the MGB GT introduced, a hardtop version of the roadster that had a hatchback-style tailgate, which made it even more practical as a touring two-seater. Chrome bumpers, leather seats, and wire wheels all added to the B's appeal, especially for overseas buyers enamored by the aura of British sports cars. Automatic transmission was offered as an option on the '67 MkII, and the bold move of using a V8 came six years later, though in light of the oil crisis and strict US emission laws, the V8 was never exported. But American safety regulations did play their part in the B's development, with the company raising the ride height and attaching ungainly rubber bumpers to the model. The result was ugly handling on an ugly car, though that didn't stop the public from buying the model in serious numbers right up until production ceased in 1980.

> **"The B was seen as a triumphant swansong for the MG brand, so much so that the MG logo was revived on later Rover models."**

Years of experience
MG had extablished a reputation for building cheap, accessible sports cars, and in the B it delivered the most successful of them all.

Viable proposition
Attacking corners at full tilt could now be accomplished more easily in the MGB, making it an attractive model for racing teams and individuals.

The celebrated MGB – a British success story

"If it ain't broke, don't fix it" may be a widely acknowledged principle, but whether it applies to sports car design is a moot point. When the MGB first appeared in 1962, BMC knew that it had a winner that would build on the huge success of the MGA. The car looked great, handled well, and delivered the level of performance that the company knew its customers wanted. Sales figures immediately confirmed that this product was right-on. Over the years, though, surely some change would have been in order? Maybe it was the failure of the MGC through its brief and unhappy existence from 1967–69, or the failure of the V8-engined version of the MGB to establish itself in the marketplace, but somewhere the will to change got lost. By 1980, although some admirers lamented its demise, the MGB had long fallen behind the cutting edge.

Front view

Rear view

Side view

Engine
The four-cylinder 1798cc block was a larger version of the B-Series engine in the MGA *(see pages 76–79)*. The 1973 V8 option used a 3532cc Rover unit made of aluminum that was actually lighter than the smaller block.

Personal touch
Steel body panels were finished by hand.

Design and Production

Model	MGB (1962–1980)
Production	512,243
Body style	Steel front-engined two seater with aluminum hood.
Construction	One piece monocoque body.
Engine	Four-cylinder, 1798cc.
Power output	92 bhp at 5400 rpm.
Transmission	Four-speed with overdrive.
Suspension	Front: independent coil; Rear: half-elliptic leaf springs.
Brakes	Lockheed discs front, drums rear.
Max speed	106 mph (171 km/h)

The investment that went into tooling up for the MGB, with its unitary pressed-steel monocoque body and chassis, could only be justified by massive sales – MG's general manager, John Thornley, is reported to have said that he knew the MGB would be the company's last new sports car the moment he saw the tooling bill. The Abingdon factory turned out almost 138,000 of the original Bs between 1962 and 1967, and over 375,000 Mark IIs from 1967 to 1980.

One sign of changing times in the marketing launch of the MGB was the increasing emphasis on safety – seat belts were even available as an optional extra. Also noticeable was the prominence of women drivers in promotional material. The kind of sales the MGB required – and got – could only be achieved by targeting the broadest possible market, therefore the stress also on the room for luggage in the trunk and children in the back.

Restricted space
(right) With the spare wheel positioned in the trunk there was only just enough room to pack a couple of small bags. Compared to the MGA's shallower, more steeply-sloped trunk, though, it was positively cavernous.

Holding the road
(left) Tweaks to the rear suspension – lever arm shocks now controlled the semi-elliptic springs – helped improve the B's ride quality over the A.

Weather protection
(left) Early cars had a "packaway" top made from ICI Everflex.

Hard body
The one-piece body was strong and roomy.

Wire option
Bolt-on wheels came as standard; wires were optional.

Vintage comfort
(right) The traditional British sports car interior consisted of a crackle black metal fascia, massive steering wheel and leather seats. An advertising campaign for the MGB GT in 1965 highlighted the use of Connolly leather "to add character to seating comfort."

CHEVROLET
CORVETTE STING RAY

Ten years after the original Corvette was released, Chevrolet announced the first major model change with the '63 Sting Ray. It was a bold design breakthrough that gave concrete expression to the many ideas of new GM styling chief Bill Mitchell. What's more, for the first time a coupé was available, though the ubiquitous split-shield coupe was panned by some of the driving press and the rear redesigned for the next model year.

Short-sighted critics aside, the '63–67 Sting Ray was a winner, with almost 120,000 of the fiberglass-bodied, V8-powered slingshots sold. And when disc brakes replaced drums in 1965 to counter the 250-plus horses, the final piece of the most complete of sports cars was in place. The Sting Ray was one of the most luscious creations ever to come out of the Chevy stable, and its success consolidated the Corvette's position as the foremost sports model in the US.

Night lights
Some Sting Rays were equipped with fog lights for night illum nation in endurance races.

King of the track
The 'Vette's wind-cheating profile gave it awesome straight-line speed.

Daytona victory
George Wintersteen wins the GT class at Daytona's 24-hour Continental race.

Holding the road
The Sting Ray's distinctive styling
was matched by superb engineering,
with a ladder frame and independent
rear suspension.

One for the road – unparalleled performance

"The Sting Ray represents leadership in automotive design. It is tomorrow's car, on the street today." That was how the editors of *Car Life* magazine saluted the arrival of the new Corvette in 1963. Road testers may have baulked at the bar that divided the rear window of the coupe version, but no one had any argument with the car's tremendous performance. Output of the V8 engines initially on offer ranged from the standard 250 bhp to 340 bhp. With a Rochester fuel-injection system, power was even more impressive. Capable of acceleration from 0–60 mph (96 km/h) in 5.6 seconds, the Sting Ray could claim to leave any other true production car in the dust. The exception was the Shelby AC Cobra *(see pages 148–51)*, which repeatedly muscled ahead of the Sting Ray in races – but which was, in Chevrolet's strongly-held opinion, not a genuine production model.

Front view

Rear view

Side view

Small block
"Big block" Sting Rays had a wider hood power bulge.

Design and Production

Model	Chevrolet Corvette Sting Ray (1966)
Production	27,720 (1966 model)
Body styles	Two-door, two-seater coupe and convertible.
Construction	Ladder frame with fiberglass body.
Engines	327cid, 427cid V8s.
Power output	300–425 bhp.
Transmission	Three-speed manual, optional four-speed manual, and two-speed Powerglide automatic.
Suspension	Front: coil springs; Rear: independent.
Brakes	Front and rear drums, optional front and rear discs.
Max speed	118–150 mph (190–241 km/h)

Development of the Corvette Sting Ray began in 1959 with the experimental XP-720. A series of challenges were presented to Chevrolet engineers, including design of a novel chassis with independent rear suspension, and hidden rotating headlights. Styling was based on a 1950s Chevrolet racer, the Stingray. Company stylists wanted to make the new Corvette a coupé-only design, but were overruled. Prototypes were subjected to extensive wind-tunnel tests to refine aerodynamics before the first 25 pilot-line Sting Rays appeared in 1962. More than 20,000 Sting Rays — almost equal numbers of coupés and roadsters — were sold in 1963, the first year of mass production, an output only possible through the working of two complete shifts a day at the St. Louis factory. Even so, purchasers faced a waiting time of about 60 days, and no discounts were needed to sell the cars.

Interior

Air conditioning was available, but very few convertible buyers chose this option; power steering was a more popular extra. Tachometer, seat belts, and electric clock came as standard. The seats were flat instead of figure-hugging, and the deep-dished, wood effect steering wheel came close to the chest.

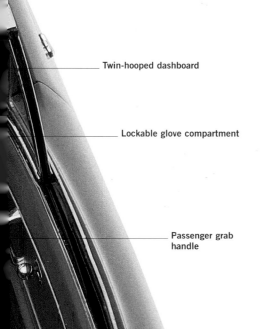

Twin-hooped dashboard

Lockable glove compartment

Passenger grab handle

Simple frame

(above) The Sting Ray's ladder chassis was uncomplicated but effective, aided by the fact that the front cross member was now welded instead of bolted on. The frame had to be strengthened when the "big block" 396 and 427cid engines were offered in 1965 and '66 respectively.

Convertible or not?

(above) Chevy's apologetic statement of "sorry, some decisions don't come easy" referred to the choice buyers had to make between the convertible and the sports coupé, with both offering "precision engineering."

Limited edition

(right) The split-shield coupe was only made in 1963, so adjustments had to be made on the '64 assembly line.

MASERATI
MISTRALE SPYDER

One of the most elegant cars of its day, the Maserati Tipo 109, better known as the Mistrale, was styled by Pietro Frua and became the last of the company's street-legal straight-sixes. Named after the wind, it was launched at the 1964 Turin Motor Show to warm approval. *Autosport*'s John Bolster said that the agonisingly pretty Spyder was "gloriously controllable and a pleasure I shall remember for a long time."

A good looker from any angle, the cockpit was very upper-crust Sixties, the Lucas injected twin-cam six could manage 150 mph (240 km/h) plus, and the tubular chassis gave commendable body control. But the glorious lines of the Spyder make the ragtop Mistrale one of Maserati's finest confections. Only 120 were ever made and they became one of the most desirable machines of the Sixties supercar set. They say looks aren't important, but in the case of the drop-top Mistrale they're absolutely everything.

Car for the star
Italian sports cars have always held an attraction for the glitterati, and the Mistrale was no exception. Here actor Alberto Sordi is pictured with his Spyder.

Exhilarating ride
The limited edition Mistrale Spyder
may have looked similar to other
sports models of the period, but its
breathtaking performance on the road
left you in no doubt it was a Maserati.

6 II E

The understated Mistrale – race heritage on the road

In the 1950s the Maserati name was synonymous with car racing, the Modena firm supplying cars driven by the likes of Stirling Moss and Juan Fangio. But by 1958 Maserati boss Omer Orsi had decided that the company should turn its attention to luxury sports road cars. The result was the 3500 series of open-tops and coupes, Maserati's first true production cars, launched in 1958. The Mistrale derived from the 3500s, with the same six-cylinder in-line engine (in a fuel-injected version) and the same basic chassis and suspension layout, but unmatchably fabulous looks. The Mistrale and its stablemates hardly made Maserati into a mass-production outfit, but growth was impressive by the firm's own standards. Whereas in the late 1950s the Modena factory turned out two cars a week, by the end of the 1960s it would be upward of two cars a day.

Front view

Rear view

Side view

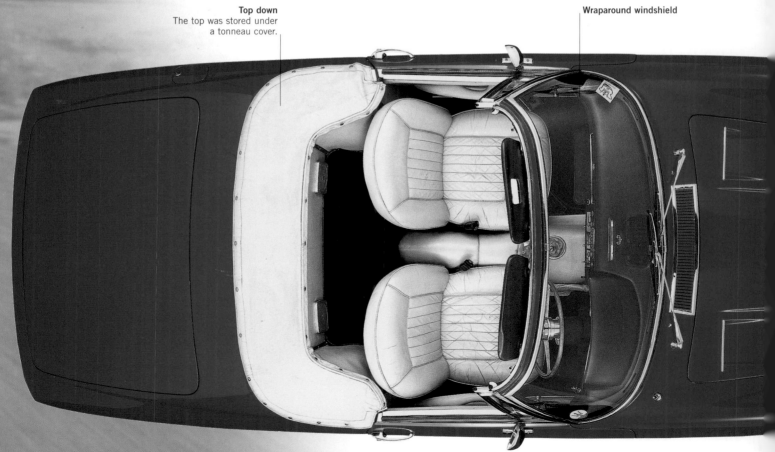

Top down
The top was stored under a tonneau cover.

Wraparound windshield

Design and Production

Model	Maserati Mistrale Spyder (1963–69)
Production	120
Body style	Two-seat convertible.
Construction	Tubular chassis, steel body.
Engines	3692cc and 4012cc six-cylinder.
Power output	245–255 bhp
Transmission	Five-speed manual.
Suspension	Front: independent with coil springs; Rear: semi-elliptic springs.
Brakes	Discs all around.
Max speed	147 mph (237 km/h)

Power bulge

The Maserati 3500 series was built around a six-cylinder inline twin-overhead-camshaft engine, derived from the 350S unit that had powered the company's race cars. For the rest of the mechanical parts Maserati made no attempt at innovation, adopting a tubular-frame chassis with coil-spring front suspension and a live rear axle with half-elliptic leaf springs – a pretty standard setup for an Italian sports car of its day. Maserati had no facilities for making its own bodywork and turned to a variety of Italian suppliers for a stylish exterior – different builders sometimes providing bodies for the same models. By 1962 the Sebring

model had joined the 3500 series. This had, among other features, fuel injection – raising engine output to 235 bhp – disc brakes, and a five-speed manual gearbox. The Mistrale Spyder and coupe appeared the following year as a further evolution from the Sebring, distinguished not only by the Frua-designed bodywork, but also by the largest versions of the Maserati six-cylinder inline engine ever produced – there was either a 3692cc block giving 245 bhp or a 4012cc monster generating 255 bhp. The Mistrale stayed in production up to 1969. In all 948 were built, 120 of them Spyder convertibles.

Flexible 'vertible
(right) The Spyder came with a soft top, but could be ordered with an optional steel hardtop. Its simple styling was similar to that of the AC models of the period that Frua was also commissioned to design.

Interior
(left) Sumptuous white leather graced the Mistrale's cockpit, not just on the seats but extending through to the transmission tunnel and insides of the doors. The wood-rim steering wheel may have been of buslike proportions, but it worked the worm and sector steering effectively.

Alternative Mistrale
(right) Frua also designed a two-door fastback coupe for the Mistrale, which was a far bigger seller than the Spyder. Both models had the same choice of inline six engines, the last time Maserati used this configuration.

1965 racer
Though sometimes criticized for having too much power in too short a wheelbase, Tigers were successful racers, and still compete today.

SUNBEAM
TIGER

"The Shelby-engineered Tiger is often dubbed 'The poor man's Cobra.'"

After achieving a few race successes early on in its life, the Sunbeam Alpine (see pages 96–99) was starting to look tame compared to other British racers such as MG. In an era where race laurels equated to production car sales, Rootes, the owners of Sunbeam, decided to boost the Alpine's image, and who better to turn to than Carroll Shelby, who had created the awesome Cobra (see pages 148–51) with AC Motors. Shelby proposed equipping the Alpine with a 4.2-liter Ford V8 and had a model delivered to him in the US so that he could work on a race version of the car. Ken Miles of Shelby-American Racing was given the task of constructing a roadgoing model. After making modifications to the chassis and suspension, the prototype was sent back to the UK in 1964, where it received the seal of approval from Rootes.

The makeover was an instant hit. The Tiger secured top spot in its class at a number of rallies in Europe – including the 1965 Monte Carlo – and achieved further notable victories in the US. The average customer was also having fun, with the production Tiger's reasonable price tag allowing Jaguar-type performance at a fraction of the cost. A 4.7-liter V8 accompanied the Mark II in 1967, but with Chrysler taking over Rootes the end was in sight for the Ford-powered Tiger, and just 571 Mark IIs were built. "The poor man's Cobra" stands out as a fine example of how British design and American horsepower could be combined to produce a highly exceptional sports car.

Driving is believing
(above) It's hard to believe that such an unassuming little sports roadster incorporated a 4-liter-plus engine and was able to hit 60 mph (96 km/h) in just 7.5 seconds.

Celebrity endorsement
(left) Often seen in a nice set of wheels, Cary Grant had the distinction of owning his Tiger, the first 1966 model to be delivered to the US.

The power-packed Tiger – Alpine in disguise

When Rootes decided to imitate the AC Cobra *(see pages 148–51)* with a "Shelby-ized" version of the Sunbeam Alpine, there was neither enough time nor enough money to engage in a restyling exercise. It was an expert's trick to spot the difference in look between the Tiger and an Alpine IV or V – a chrome strip along the flanks and double exhaust outlets were the giveaway signs. But driving the car would leave no one in any doubt. The Tiger's performance matched its name, the Ford unit providing about double the bhp of the Alpine's powerplant. Chrysler's negative attitude toward producing and marketing a car with a Ford engine brought development of the Tiger to an abrupt end in 1967. A plan to continue Tiger production with a Chrysler V8 unit was abandoned when it turned out that this more cumbersome engine was too heavy and, in any case, wouldn't fit.

Front view

Rear view

Side view

Engine
Early Tigers used 4.2-liter Ford blocks, but performance options – especially in the US – soon became available and included four-barrel Holley carburetors. The bigger 4.7-liter unit put out an astounding 200 bhp.

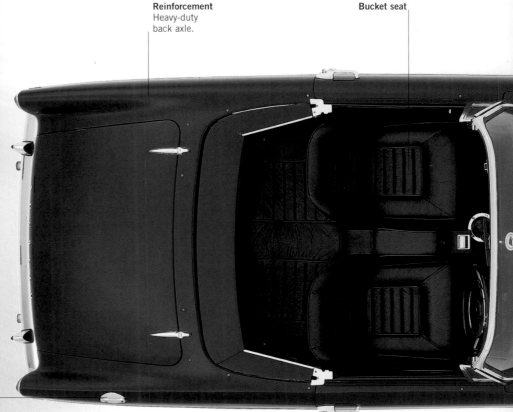

Reinforcement
Heavy-duty back axle.

Bucket seat

Thirsty Tiger
Not surprisingly, the Tiger guzzled fuel, at the rate of 20 mpg (7 km/l).

Design and Production

Model	Sunbeam Tiger (1964–67)
Production	Mk1 (1964–67): 6,496; MkII (1967): 571.
Body style	Two-plus-two roadster.
Construction	Steel monocoque.
Engines	Ford V8 4261cc and 4727cc (260/289cid).
Power output	164 bhp at 4400 rpm (4261cc), 200 bhp at 4400 rpm (4727cc).
Transmission	Four-speed manual.
Suspension	Front: coil springs and wishbones; Rear: rigid axle on semi-elliptic leaf springs.
Brakes	Servo-assisted front discs, rear drums.
Max speed	117 mph (188 km/h) (4261cc), 125 mph (201 km/h) (4727cc)

The initial engineering to adapt the Sunbeam Alpine to the Ford V8 engine was carried out by Carroll Shelby in California. Although compact, the V8 unit could only just be put under the Alpine's hood, set back toward the bulkhead. Shelby shipped the resulting one-off prototype to Rootes in Coventry for approval and it was then put into production in Britain. The differences between the Tiger and the Alpine, at least under the body, were sufficient to deter Rootes from giving the job to its existing Alpine assembly lines at Ryton-on-Dunsmore. Instead, production was subcontracted to Jensen Motors in West Bromwich, which was already making body for Austin-Healey 3000s as well as its own cars. When Tigers started rolling off the production line in 1964, they were all shipped out to the US. The car did not go on sale in its country of origin until the following year. The 1967 Mark II was marketed exclusively in the US. In all, 7,044 Tigers had been built by the time production ended in 1967.

Roar of the Tiger
(left) While it may have been presented as an ideal car for the average couple, the Tiger's beefy blocks meant it was more renowned as a race vehicle. Besides some European rally wins, it was most at home on the road-racing circuits of the US.

Alpine modifications
(below) The Alpine's transmission was uprated to a T-10 on the Tiger and rack-and-pinion steering replaced the circulating-ball gear.

Revised hood
Racing Tigers had a raised hood to improve airflow.

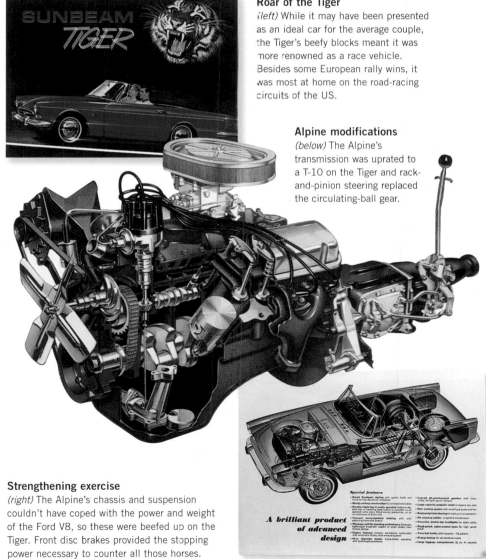

Strengthening exercise
(right) The Alpine's chassis and suspension couldn't have coped with the power and weight of the Ford V8, so these were beefed up on the Tiger. Front disc brakes provided the stopping power necessary to counter all those horses.

AC COBRA 427

Carroll Shelby wanted one thing more than anything else – to win Le Mans. The Texan racer set up the Shelby-American racing team, but with little initial success. The problem was that the Ferraris were still unbeatable and Ford wasn't willing to put up money for a racing project. The solution was found in a traditional British car maker, AC Cars, with its Ace forming the basis for the Cobra. Shelby started off by shoe-horning in 4.2- and 4.7-litre Mustang engines, but the showpiece came along in 1967 – the Cobra 427.

With an aluminium body wrapped around a tubular steel frame, the 427 was light yet strong. And it needed to be, with the 7-litre powerplant pushing out 425 bhp. Despite dazzling performance, the Cobra never won Le Mans and production wound down as Shelby devoted more time to other projects. But the few owners of this big-block Cobra could find consolation in having bought one of the most brutish motoring legends ever built.

Suitable frame
The big-block Cobra needed a revised chassis to cope with the 427cid powerplant and was fitted with a frame three times stronger than the 289's.

More gusto
(below) Racing Cobras usually had side exhausts, which increased power and noise.

Getting a grip
(below right) Cobras were always shod in Goodyear tyres as Shelby was a long-time dealer of the brand.

Early successes
August 1964 was a good month for Cobras in Europe, with podium finishes at events in the Black Forest, Switzerland, and here at the Goodwood TT.

The mighty 427 – largest of the Cobras

Carroll Shelby is on record as saying in 1964: "I build Cobras with my heart rather than for a profit." He wanted to race the cars, not sell them. The progressive development of the car away from its origins in the Ace was all to do with feedback from competition experience and with the goal of increasing competition performance. Major improvements included the introduction of rack-and-pinion steering, and coil-spring suspension to replace leaf-spring suspension. The most visible change involved the wheelarches designed to accommodate extra-large tires. The engine, though, was clearly the most important line of development, from the original 4.2-liter unit to 4.7 liters, and finally 7 liters. By 1967, the 427 had very little in common with the original 289 of 1962 – shared features were limited to the doors and hood, and not much else.

Front view   Rear view

Side view

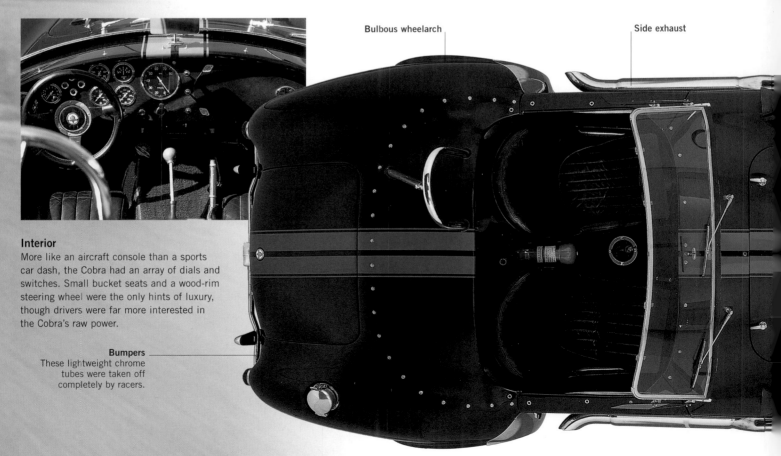

Bulbous wheelarch   Side exhaust

Interior
More like an aircraft console than a sports car dash, the Cobra had an array of dials and switches. Small bucket seats and a wood-rim steering wheel were the only hints of luxury, though drivers were far more interested in the Cobra's raw power.

Bumpers
These lightweight chrome tubes were taken off completely by racers.

Design and Production

Model	AC Cobra 427 (1965–68)
Production	356
Body style	Light alloy, two-door, two-seat, open sports.
Construction	Separate tubular steel chassis with aluminum panels.
Engine	6989cc V8.
Power output	425 bhp at 6000 rpm.
Transmission	Four-speed, all-synchromesh.
Suspension	All-around independent with coil springs.
Brakes	Discs all around.
Max speed	165 mph (265 km/h)

In early 1962 Carroll Shelby shipped two 4.2-liter Ford engines to the AC factory at Thames Ditton in England, where they were mounted into AC Aces, creating the first prototype Cobras. Production began later in the year, when a first batch of 100 AC-built bodies and chassis were dispatched to Shelby American in Los Angeles for engine installation and finishing. This original batch of Cobra 289s constituted the minimum number Shelby needed for homologation.

Production continued to be split between Britain and the US throughout the relatively brief life of the 289 and its successor the 427, leaving doubt as to the nationality to be assigned to the Cobras, as well as their designation. In the US the cars were known as Shelby American Cobras or, more loosely, Ford Cobras. Total production between 1962 and 1968 eventually reached 1,011, of which 356 were 427s with the 7-liter engine.

Aluminium bodywork

World-renowned
(above) The Cobra featured in a series of car stamps from the Caribbean island of Nevis.

Power king
(above) Carroll Shelby spent much of his life developing high-performance sports cars, though the Cobra is his most memorable project.

Engine
(left) The 427 unit had years of NASCAR (National Association of Stock Car Automobile Racing) experience, with souped-up versions capable of 500 bhp.

Baby Cobra
(above) Even the smaller-block 4.7-litre Cobras could hit 60 mph (96 km/h) in under six seconds and reach 222 km/h (138 mph).

DATSUN
FAIRLADY 1600

First exhibited at the 1961 Tokyo Motor Show, the Datsun Fairlady was a stylish offering from a Japanese car industry, which at the time was not known for manufacturing good-looking models. With a "European" profile not unlike the MGB that would come out a year later *(see pages 132–35)*, the original Fairlady was powered by a 1500cc pushrod unit incorporating a single Hitachi carb, and was no great mover. One quirk of the first Fairladys is that they were three-seaters; a small, sideways-facing seat was positioned behind the driver's seat, though many owners removed them to make more space for storing luggage.

Aimed primarily at the export market – few came to Europe, and it was never listed in the UK – the Fairlady notched up a few thousand sales in the US, where it got a reputation for being able to handle itself on racetracks. Numbers were boosted as Datsun refined the car and raised its power output so that by 1967, twin-carb, two-liter models could reach 125 mph (200 km/h). Though production figures were generally low, Datsun had gained invaluable experience in producing a sports car for the world market, and this would stand the company in good stead when the next model was rolled out. By the time the 240Z was flying out of showrooms, the public had all but forgotten the Fairlady; but this pretty car had served a useful purpose and provided the foundation for the 240Z's phenomenal success.

Tool of the trade
As an indication of how quickly the Fairlady gained respect among professionals, ex-Ferrari Formula One driver Bob Bindurant used the model to teach aspiring racers at his driving school in the mid-Sixties.

"The Fairlady's handling was poised and surefooted, endearing the car to amateur and professional racers."

Overseas competitions
The Datsun racing team was set up in 1966, using Fairladys to ccmpete in SCCA events across the US. Dan Parkinson, pictured, was its top driver.

The full-spec Fairlady – setting new standards

If you were asked to trace the origins of the Fairlady's attractive styling, you would probably have to say that it was done for them by MG. Like many companies entering a new area, Nissan chose to imitate the successful product that it wanted to compete with. The company marketed the Datsun 1600 as "the quality-minded sports car for economy-minded people." The sales pitch was clear and sensible: this might not be the greatest car in the world, but it is a better car than you can get anywhere else for the price. One of the Datsun's crucial selling points was the amount of equipment that came as standard with the 1600 but was at that time still specified by many other companies as "optional extras." This included a transistor radio, seat belts, racing steering wheel, heater, windshield wipers, and whitewall tires.

Front view

Rear view

Side view

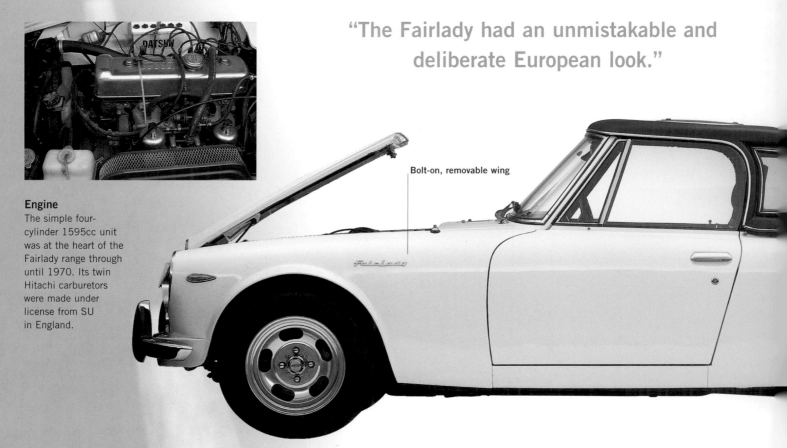

Engine
The simple four-cylinder 1595cc unit was at the heart of the Fairlady range through until 1970. Its twin Hitachi carburetors were made under license from SU in England.

"The Fairlady had an unmistakable and deliberate European look."

Bolt-on, removable wing

Design and Production

Model	Datsun Fairlady 1600 (1965–70)
Production	Approx 40,000
Body style	Two-seater sports convertible.
Construction	Steel body mounted on box-section chassis.
Engine	1595cc four-cylinder.
Power output	90 bhp at 6000 rpm.
Transmission	Four-speed all-synchro.
Suspension	Front: independent; Rear: leaf springs.
Brakes	Front discs, rear drums.
Max speed	105 mph (169 km/h)

Although Nissan resumed production in 1947 after the traumas of World War II, it was not finally freed from restrictions imposed by the American occupying authorities until 1955. The company's growth strategy was necessarily export-oriented and it began penetration of the American market in the 1960s. Nissan was going through a phase of rapid expansion of its manufacturing base at the time the 1600 was in production, opening new plants at Oppama and Zama, and acquiring the Murayama plant through a merger with Prince Motors. The Japanese had in their favor a dedicated, relatively low-wage workforce, engineering know-how, good quality control, and an open-minded facility for responding to the tastes and needs of foreign consumers. The Fairlady was a modest success in terms of sales – around 40,000 were produced. But it paved the way for future triumphs. In the following decade, Americans would in no uncertain measure get used to the initially unfamiliar idea of owning a Japanese-made sports car as the Datsun 240Z swept to world dominance.

Prototype planning
(right) Hidehiro Iizuka was commissioned to design a prototype of a car that Datsun could sell overseas. His early sketches show that the production model was similar to the initial concept.

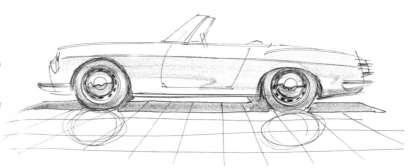

Neat trick
The hood folded down behind the seats.

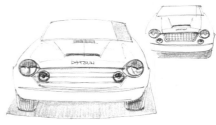

Racy lady
(left) As well as being excellent value-for-money, the Fairlady's performance was promoted in slightly sketchy copy: "Grab the racing-type steering wheel and get set for an exciting new experience in sports car driving."

Shore to ship
(right) For the first time in the Japanese car-making industry, plants such as Nissan's port-side Yokohama facility were gearing up for export. The Fairlady was a dry run for the far busier foreign sales that lay ahead.

AC 428

Combining British engineering, American power, and Italian design was always going to create an interesting end product, and the AC 428 proved that the mix really could work. The October 1965 London Motor Show saw the convertible make its debut, with the fixed–head – fastback – version released at the Geneva Motor Show five months later. Initial reaction to the car was positive, the model's elegant lines belying the frightening power under the hood from a V8 that could push out a staggering 345 horses and knock on the door of 140 mph (225 km/h).

On paper – and in the flesh – the 428 had everything going for it, not least the elegant design by Pietro Frua of Turin and a chassis based on the legendary Cobra 427 *(see pages 148–51)*. But from the outset all was not well on the production front, with the first cars not actually offered for sale until 1967; two years later a measly 50 complete models had been manufactured. This was no surprise when you consider that the car was essentially made in three countries, with the engine imported into the UK from the US and the chassis then being sent on to Italy. A pricing policy that placed the 428 between the cheaper British Astons and Jensens and more expensive Italian Ferraris and Maseratis didn't help, so that by the time the last one dribbled out of the factory in 1973 only 80 had been built. This was a shame, since there were many positive attributes to a beautiful bruiser that was one of the few attempts by a European manufacturer to produce its own version of a US "muscle" car.

Essential discs
(below) Though a "refined" sports cruiser, there was still plenty of power under the hood and dual circuit disc brakes helped calm the driver's nerves.

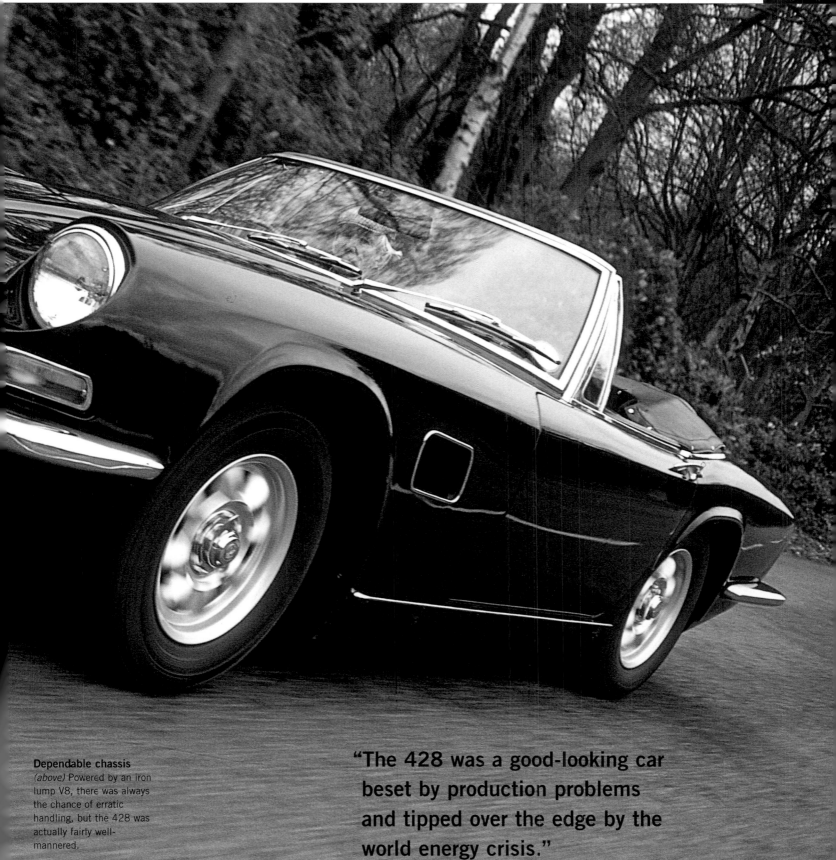

Dependable chassis
(above) Powered by an iron lump V8, there was always the chance of erratic handling, but the 428 was actually fairly well-mannered.

"The 428 was a good-looking car beset by production problems and tipped over the edge by the world energy crisis."

The rare 428 – performance–luxury hybrid

The AC 428 was an attempt to exploit the renown of the Cobra *(see pages 148–51)* with a follow-up that would be a sophisticated and powerful road car rather than a scary white-knuckle racer. Italian builder Frua was making bodies for the Maserati Mistrale *(see pages 140–43)* in the 1960s, and, asked to perform the same service for the AC 428, not surprisingly came up with an extremely similar look – even making possible some economical sharing of panels between the two cars. But the AC 428 was no lightweight. The heavy cast-iron Ford engine at the front was well matched by the weight of all the steel behind it. And the Ford unit had the muscle to accelerate this load to 100 mph (161 km/h) from a standing start in 14.5 seconds – some of the more exciting seconds in life if you ever got the chance to do it.

Front view

Rear view

Side view

Engine
AC used the same 427cid block in the car as in the Cobra, so it was originally known as the AC 427. In 1967 the Ford Galaxie unit was installed, providing the extra cubic inch. Overheating was a problem on many early 428s, rectified to a certain degree by the addition of air vents behind the front wheels.

Front opening
Like the Cobra, the 428's hood was hinged at the front.

Thin-skinned
Early cars had aluminum doors and hood; later versions were all-steel.

Design and Production

Model	AC 428 (1966–73)
Production	80 (51 convertibles, 29 fastbacks)
Body styles	Two-seat convertible or two-seat fastback coupe.
Construction	Tubular-steel backbone chassis/separate all-steel body.
Engines	6997cc or 7016cc Ford V8.
Power output	345 bhp at 4600 rpm.
Transmission	Ford four-speed manual or three-speed auto; Salisbury rear axle with limited-slip differential.
Suspension	Double wishbones and combined coil spring/telescopic damper units front and rear.
Brakes	Servo-assisted Girling discs front and rear.
Max speed	139 mph (224 km/h)

Thirsty beast
The 428 drank gas at the rate of 15 mpg (5.3 km/l).

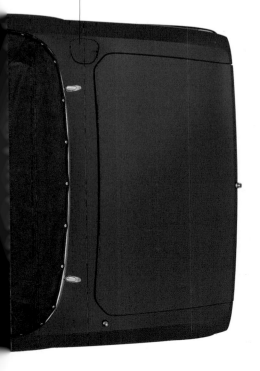

The 428 used a slightly elongated version of the AC 427 Cobra's tubular chassis and the same coil-spring suspension. Like the Cobra, it was equipped with a Ford engine, the 7016cc (428cid) V8 from the Galaxie. The 428's unit was actually larger than the Cobra's 6996cc (427cid) unit – hence the two cars' respective designations – but it was less highly tuned. The convoluted production process for the AC 428 was a logistical nightmare. The Ford running gear had to be shipped over from Detroit to Thames Ditton, England, then the rolling chassis forwarded to Frua in Turin where the bodies were attached and finished, and finally the cars sent back to Thames Ditton for completion. Getting bodies out of Frua proved exceptionally difficult, the fraught state of industrial relations in Italy at the time doing nothing to help an already cumbersome process. Production slowed and costs necessarily escalated. Eight years after the original 1965 prototype, only 80 more AC 428s had been built.

Classy appeal
(left) AC attempted to woo those with more money than sense, but was soon found out. Buyers were going to look very hard at a car costing more than an Aston DB6, and upon close inspection the 428 lacked the necessary refinements.

Interior
(right) Looking much like a compact version of an aircraft flightdeck, the AC's many dials were positioned clearly in front of the driver. Leather seats and chrome fixtures created a certain air of luxury, though the cockpit felt a little claustrophobic with the top up.

Body trouble
(left) The 428's body panels were designed and built by Frua, though the quality of the Italian steel was poor and vulnerable to corrosion. This went some way to explaining the painfully slow production process, with AC not able to secure enough high standard steel to make a regular flow of cars.

The Seventies

"The Seventies did for sports cars what Richard Nixon did for truth."

THE REGULATED YEARS

1970

Given the incredible popularity of the sports car in the Sixties, we shouldn't have been surprised when things suddenly started to go wrong. Cars, like most other consumer goods, are constantly changed by fashion. But the dark storm clouds growing on the horizon weren't just due to a shift in customer demand. The new-age sports sedan and executive express may have been taking their toll on sales, but the aspirational two-seater could have survived the Seventies had it not been for an unprecedented wave of political, environmental, and safety legislation.

Two severe worldwide energy crises didn't help the fortunes of gas guzzlers like the V12 E-Type *(see pages 184–87)*, MGB V8, and Chevrolet Corvette. Large-capacity engines suddenly became a social liability. But the greatest damage was done by the US government's perception that the convertible was essentially one of the most dangerous body configurations available. And no amount of roll bars or body stiffening would help. Both driver and passenger were considered vulnerable. While the US legislators didn't actually ban the open-top outright, they insisted that to be sold in the American market it must conform to a litany of new safety regulations, which added huge production costs.

Timeline 1970s

1970	1971	1972	1973	1974
• Burt Bacharach shoots to fame with his song, *Raindrops Keep Falling On My Head*.	• A postal strike halts mail delivery in Britain for 47 days.	• The Watergate scandal begins with the arrest of five men inside the Democratic National Headquarters in the Watergate complex.	• The British government orders a three-day working week to conserve electricity following a coal strike.	**Lotus Elan**
• The Triumph Stag is launched to wide acclaim.	• Jaguar unveils its redesigned E-Type Series III with a V12 in the line.	• A coal strike lasting 47 days cripples Britain.	• The MG GT V8 is launched.	• The Lamborghini Countach is produced with the aim of challenging Ferrari's domination of the supercar market.
Alfa Romeo Spider	• An earthquake in Los Angeles kills 60 people and causes $1 billion damage.	• Britain imposes direct rule on Northern Ireland.		• The Porsche 911 Turbo is introduced.
• Floods kill half a million people in East Pakistan.	• Riots and violence in Northern Ireland escalate.	• Britain agrees to full membership of the European Economic Community (EEC).		• Daylight Saving Time is adopted in the US to save on fuel consumption.
• The South African cricket tour of Britain is cancelled.	• *Fiddler on the Roof* becomes the longest-running musical in the history of Broadway.	• The first oil crisis starts in the US.		
	• Rolls Royce Ltd. declares bankruptcy.	• Arab terrorists kill two Israeli Olympic athletes in Munich.	**Morgan logo**	
	• India and Pakistan go to war after India supports Bengali rebels.			

THE EFFECTS OF INTERVENTION

Just getting any car through the new federal safety standard was expensive enough, but on sports cars the cost turned out to be prohibitive. And that's why so many Seventies sports models looked so ungainly. Higher bumpers and headlights often meant different ride heights, which played havoc with carefully balanced suspension settings. So not only did the MGB now look awful, but it handled badly too. Inevitable cost-cutting by the manufacturers followed and build quality dived. Sporadic industry strikes also took their toll and cars like the Triumph TR6 (see pages 172–75), Jensen-Healey (see pages 192–95),

Alfa Spider, and Jaguar XJS, were plagued by indifferent and sometimes atrocious quality control.

The budget, accessible sports car became an endangered species as carmakers switched their attention to performance sedans. With the profitable US market gone, alfresco driving now came at a price as only specialized companies could afford to offer soft-tops. But it was a malaise that went on to affect the whole industry. Labor costs spiraled, engineering integrity declined, and the once-great individualism and creativity of car design ebbed slowly away. We'll always remember the Seventies as a decade of ghastly clothes and hairstyles, but if truth be told the cars were pretty grim too.

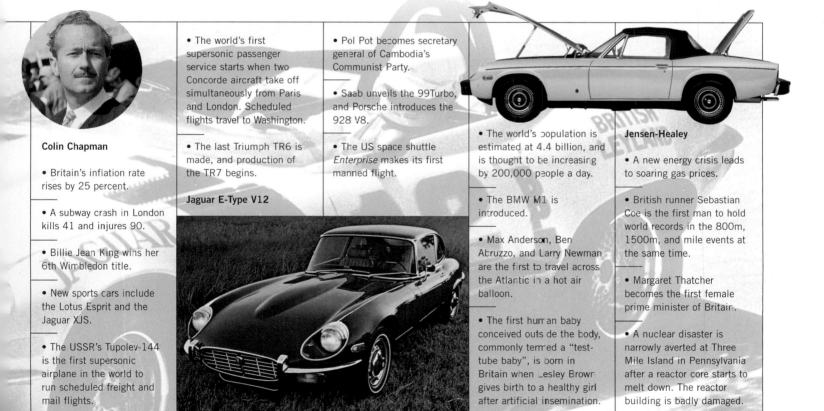

Colin Chapman

- Britain's inflation rate rises by 25 percent.
- A subway crash in London kills 41 and injures 90.
- Billie Jean King wins her 6th Wimbledon title.
- New sports cars include the Lotus Esprit and the Jaguar XJS.
- The USSR's Tupolev-144 is the first supersonic airplane in the world to run scheduled freight and mail flights.

1975

- The world's first supersonic passenger service starts when two Concorde aircraft take off simultaneously from Paris and London. Scheduled flights travel to Washington.
- The last Triumph TR6 is made, and production of the TR7 begins.

Jaguar E-Type V12

1976

- Pol Pot becomes secretary general of Cambodia's Communist Party.
- Saab unveils the 99Turbo, and Porsche introduces the 928 V8.
- The US space shuttle Enterprise makes its first manned flight.

1977

- The world's population is estimated at 4.4 billion, and is thought to be increasing by 200,000 people a day.
- The BMW M1 is introduced.
- Max Anderson, Ben Abruzzo, and Larry Newman are the first to travel across the Atlantic in a hot air balloon.
- The first human baby conceived outside the body, commonly termed a "test-tube baby", is born in Britain when Lesley Brown gives birth to a healthy girl after artificial insemination.

1978

Jensen-Healey

- A new energy crisis leads to soaring gas prices.
- British runner Sebastian Coe is the first man to hold world records in the 800m, 1500m, and mile events at the same time.
- Margaret Thatcher becomes the first female prime minister of Britain.
- A nuclear disaster is narrowly averted at Three Mile Island in Pennsylvania after a reactor core starts to melt down. The reactor building is badly damaged.

1979

ALFA ROMEO
1300 JUNIOR SPIDER

One of the most instantly likeable Italian cars, the Alfa Romeo Duetto Spider was launched at the 1966 Geneva Motor Show. In a shrewd marketing ploy, Alfa had held a competition to come up with a name for its new model, and among the 140,000 entries were suggestions such as Bardot, Lollobridgida, and even Stalin. The company went for Duetto, which was hard to argue with considering this was a two-seater. And how would signor and signori find the car as they took it out into the hills for a romantic weekend? With a wonderfully responsive all-alloy, twin-cam engine, accurate steering, sensitive brakes, and a finely balanced chassis. And with styling by Pininfarina to round things off, it all added up to a neat little sports tourer.

Priced at the same level as Jaguar's faster and more glamourous E-Type *(see pages 124–27)*, the Spider didn't come cheap, and in 1968 Alfa decided to offer a smaller-engined version of the original 1570cc Duetto – the 1300 Junior Spider. The baby of the Spider family may have pushed out 20 horses less than the Duetto – and nearly 30 fewer than the simultaneously released 1750 Spider Veloce – but it retained the matinee idol looks. Styling on all Spiders changed in 1970 when the "boat-tail" rear was replaced by a squared-off tail. Though Alfa purists would insist the post-'70 design is inferior, it was a square-tailed model – the 2000 Spider Veloce – which sold more than any other, with over 80,000 made right up to 1994. As for the 1300 Junior, it lived on until 1978.

Lure of the Spider
The Milanese-produced Alfa Spider was, according to the advertising material, a car for lovers of life, and stylish young things with plenty of spare lira soon bought them up.

Design connection
With Pininfarina
designing for both
manufacturers, the
Alfa Spider has often
been dubbed "the
poor man's Ferrari."

Alfa's solid Junior – baby of the family

The 1960s was the decade of youth culture, and Alfa Romeo predictably played on the youth theme in the sales pitch for the aptly named "Junior" 1300 Spider, GT, and GTA models. "Three sports cars for 20-year-olds of all ages" trumpeted the promotional literature, although it is hard to believe there were many youngsters actually of that age who could stump up the price of these wonderful cars – even if they were a little less fabulously expensive than the original Duetto. With performance almost taken for granted, comfort and looks were the selling points. Alfa boasted that soundproofing had reduced noise in the passenger compartment to the level found in sedan cars and was also eager to point out the size of the trunk, making this a truly practical car for a couple on vacation. This was, in short, definitely a grown-up tourer.

Front view

Rear view

Side view

" Alfa's racing heritage gave it the ability to squeeze 106 mph (170 km/h) out of the 1300cc block."

Rain protection
The top was effective and folded back neatly.

Design and Production

Model	Alfa Romeo 1300 Junior Spider (1968–78)
Production	7,237
Body style	Two-door, two-seater.
Construction	All-steel monocoque body.
Engine	All-alloy twin-cam 1290cc.
Power output	89 bhp at 6000 rpm.
Transmission	Five-speed.
Suspension	Front: independent; Rear: live axle with coil springs.
Brakes	Discs all around.
Max speed	106 mph (170 km/h)

The styling of the Duetto series was Italian design guru Battista Farina's swan song – he died in 1966, the year the car first appeared. The look was a masterpiece of elegance and restraint, even if the rounded rear end failed to please some customers (some found it challenging to park) and had eventually to be abandoned for a square-tailed look. The Pininfarina company built the bodies as well as designing them. The Junior was a variant of the Duetto, which was itself one of a variety of similar 1960s–'70s Alfas derived from the Giulietta. All these models had many features in common, including five-speed manual transmissions, coil-spring suspensions, and live rear axles. They were all powered by variants of the classic Alfa four-cylinder twin-cam engine. Sharing mechanical components inevitably brought economies of scale for the Alfa Romeo operation, while the sometimes positively confusing proliferation of minor variations on a theme was presumably believed to cover all bases on the sports car market. There could certainly be no arguing with the numbers in which they sold.

Driving position
(right) All Spider cockpits were designed with the Italian apelike driving position – long arms and short legs.

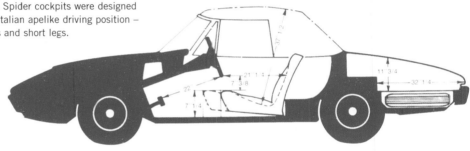

Fuel consumption
With a figure of 29 mpg (10.3 km/l), the Junior Spider was pretty frugal.

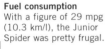

Interior
(left) Deep seats and quality upholstery were Alfa trademarks. Fingertip stalks operated minor controls and a nifty foot button controlled the windshield wipers. A Pininfarina badge on the dash reminded drivers they were sitting in a refined vehicle.

Adaptable Alfa
(right) Alfa literature promoted the Junior Spider as having the flexibility to handle both urban and highway driving conditions with ease. It followed, then, that the huge trunk could carry shopping bags or suitcases.

Smile... it's a Morgan
So traditional it's almost quirky, the Morgan has featured in a number of movies. Here it's starring alongside Marty Feldman and Mel Brooks in the 1976 production *Silent Movie*.

MORGAN
PLUS EIGHT

Like so many great British sports cars, the fastest Morgan was born by accident. In the late '60s Morgan was using Triumph TR4 engines for its top-of-the-line Plus Four (see pages 52–55). But by '66 Triumph had fitted its new TR5 with a bigger six-pot unit, which wouldn't fit in the Morgan engine bay. At the time, Rover was trying to buy Morgan, and during discussions its new Buick-derived 3.5 V8 was mentioned. Peter Morgan asked if he could try shoe-horning one into a Plus Four. Surprisingly Rover said yes. In 1967 Morgan built the first Plus Eight prototype for less than $8,400 (£3,000). The Rover alloy V8 was a sweet-spinning gem of an engine, transforming the previously rather sedate Plus Four into a screaming banshee. The automotive press loved the Plus Eight's tail-happy handling and rumbling exhaust note, and soon Morgan was offering a sports lightweight version, fuel injection, and a five-speed gearbox.

With only 11 Plus Eights built a week, buyers sat on a waiting list for years. Places on the list changed hands on the black market for up to $14,000 (£5,000). Other car owners wondered what all the fuss was about. What they didn't realize was that despite the aerodynamics of a cathedral, the sober-looking Plus Eight could actually accelerate quicker than a Jag E-Type (see pages 124–27), Ferrari 330GT, or Maserati Ghibli. Suddenly all those jokes about bearded men in flat caps and woolly sweaters stopped, and the fastest Morgan ever became a highly respected and ultradesirable cult car.

Still turning heads
Always a driver's car, with fantastic levels of grip and a surefooted ride, in Plus Eight guise the Morgan is even more exciting. Though you'll have to wait up to two years to get your hands on a new one.

"The Morgan company must be doing something right if it can drop a 4-liter V8 into a frame that hasn't changed for over 60 years."

The Plus Eight – bigger engine, same style

The Morgan company has always revelled in its conservatism, so the idea of putting the latest Rover V8 into one of its cars was bold and innovative. Few other companies would have done it without changing other aspects of the car. Morgan's decision to keep the aerodynamically unsound Plus Four shape, as well as the traditional bodywork of ash hardwood frames and steel panels, created an utterly desirable blend of up-to-date power and old-fashioned style. Morgan boasts that, in the Plus Eight, the Rover engine has achieved a record for the longest continuous use of the same unit in the same car. Despite its traditionalist image the company has never been closed to innovation. Its new year 2000 model, the aluminum-bodied Aero 8, not only had a BMW V8 instead of the Rover unit, but achieved 40 percent less drag than the Plus Eight without abandoning the traditional Morgan look.

Front view

Rear view

Side view

Cubby hole
A few small items could be stored behind the seats.

Lugagge rack

Wider car
The Plus Eight's wheels were set farther apart than those on the Plus Four.

Design and Production

Model	Morgan Plus Eight (1968–)
Production	N/A
Body style	Two-seater convertible.
Construction	Alloy body, ash wood frame.
Engines	3528cc and 3946 V8s.
Power output	155–190 bhp.
Transmission	Four/five-speed manual.
Suspension	Front: independent with coil springs; Rear: semi-elliptic leaf springs.
Brakes	Front disc, rear drum.
Max speed	120-130 mph (193–209 km/h)

In equipping the Plus Four with the new 3.5-liter engine, Morgan tried to keep as much as possible of the previous model intact. The Plus Eight retained the distinctive Z-section ladder frame chassis, handcrafted bodywork, and even the antiquated Moss four-speed gearbox. The chassis had to be lengthened by about 2 in (5 cm) and there were new light alloy wheels – that was all. Over subsequent years, though, Morgan showed itself adept at discreetly adopting modern features. A Rover gearbox replaced the Moss in 1972, upgraded to five-speed from 1977. Rack-and-pinion steering was adopted in 1986. And Rover went on supplying updated versions of the engine – with fuel injection from 1984, and capacity increased to 3.9 liters in 1989. But the scale and style of manufacture at the Malvern plant remained sternly conservative. In 1999 Morgan was producing 11 cars a week – its highest output since before WWII!

Suspension
(right) The Eight retained the Four's independent front suspension, as seen here, with the two main and rebound springs attached to the steering rack. Morgans were known for their hard but stable ride.

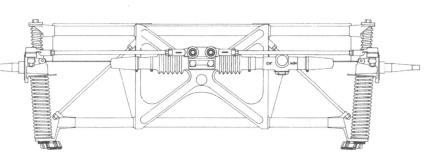

Traditional underpinnings
(left) Morgan's legendary hand-built ash frame was used in the Eight and still holds current models together, including the Aero 8. The company has found the wooden chassis to be consistently flexible and strong.

Moving on
(right) While engine access has always been good across the Morgan line, with the center-hinged hood allowing easy maintenance, the powerplants themselves have moved up a notch or two; the 2002 Plus Eight is powered by a 4-liter, 16-valve V8. Other changes on the model include aluminum superform fenders and the ultimate concession to modernity, airbags.

TRIUMPH TR6

Though Triumph would release one more model in the TR series, it's easy to see why enthusiasts consider the TR6 to be the final flourish of this long line of British sports cars. At its 1968 launch, buyers were presented with the culmination of previous TR developments, but with a modern twist. The body was based on the TR4 and had been given to Karmann to weave their magic, while under the hood the smooth six-cylinder engine had already proved its reliability in the TR5.

In 1973, the TR6 was reined in by a 25 bhp cut in power output, but the fuel-injected British model still had more punch than the carbureted American version. American buyers weren't complaining, and less than 10 percent of cars stayed in the UK. The TR6 came to the end of its life in 1976, by which time it had become the biggest selling of all the TR models, including the TR7 which was to follow – the sight of which must have had purists wishing Triumph had continued making the TR6 instead.

"Though a British sports model, the TR6's Karmann-designed body gave it a continental edge that made it stand out from its competitors."

Lively performer
The TR6 enjoyed plenty of success on the track, particularly in the US, where it still competes in various vintage auto racing events.

Spacious tourer
With more cockpit space than earlier TRs, a larger capacity trunk, and an improved driving position, the TR6 was a great all-around sports tourer.

The triumphant TR6 – a glorious swan song

The original idea for a cheap and economical sports car, which led Standard–Triumph's Sir John Black to launch the TR series in 1952, was carried through by the TR6 with a thoroughly intelligent conservatism. The TR6 had nothing to do with fashionable notions such as unit construction, sticking to a separate chassis like its predecessors, but the straight–six fuel-injected engine gave power and performance a TR2 owner would have gawked at. American buyers never benefited from this because of exhaust emissions legislation, which necessitated a version with carburetors in place of fuel injection. But they still appreciated the car's sharp style and relatively economical fuel consumption, increasingly important after gasoline price hikes in the early 1970s. The TR6 may have been far from the cutting edge of automotive progress, but it did its job.

Front view

Rear view

Side view

Export block
US models had carburetors instead of fuel injection.

Comfortable seating

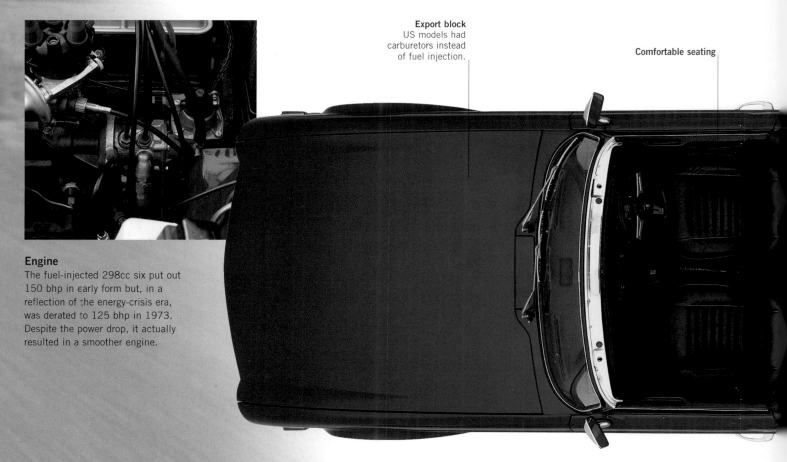

Engine
The fuel-injected 298cc six put out 150 bhp in early form but, in a reflection of the energy-crisis era, was derated to 125 bhp in 1973. Despite the power drop, it actually resulted in a smoother engine.

Design and Production

Model	Triumph TR6 (1969–76)
Production	94,619
Body style	Two-seater convertible.
Construction	Ladder-type chassis with integral steel body.
Engines	Inline six-cylinder, 2498cc, fuel-injection (carburetors in US).
Power output	152 bhp at 5500 rpm (1969–1973), 125 bhp at 5250 rpm (1973–1975), 104 bhp at 4500 rpm (US).
Transmission	Manual four-speed with optional overdrive on third and top.
Suspension	Front: independent, wishbones; Rear: independent, swing-axles & semi-trailing arms.
Brakes	Front disc, rear drums.
Max speed	119 mph (191 km/h, 150 bhp), 107 mph (172 km/h, US)

Fuel cap
The TR6 consumed petrol at the rate of 25 mpg (8.8 km/l).

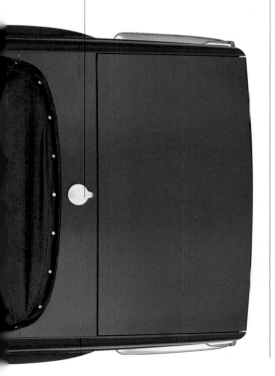

In the 1950s, the Triumph TR2 and TR3 established themselves as attractive cars at the cheaper end of the sports car market, and through the following decade, Triumph very successfully developed the series, not just maintaining but expanding its appeal. The 1962 TR4 initially involved little more than a change of look, the Michelotti-designed body giving a distinctly "modern" look to what was essentially a 1950s car – although there was also rack-and-pinion steering and an all-synchromesh transmission. The TRA of 1965 introduced the first serious mechanical innovation with semi-trailing link independent rear suspension. Next came a new engine. In 1967, the short-lived TR5 appeared with a 2.5-liter straight-six, available with Lucas fuel injection. The TR6 incorporated these advances, but with fresh body from the German firm Karmann. Between 1968 and 1976, it became the best-selling of the TR series.

TR6 line
(left) Most postwar Triumphs, including the TR6, were assembled at Standard Motor Company's plant in Canley, Coventry, England. Even working flat out, the factory found it hard to meet the high demand for the model, especially from the US.

Interior
(right) The simple dash with easy-to-read dials – a speedometer and tachometer were the main ones – was more refined than earlier TRs. A stubby gear stick emphasized the 6's sports character.

Safety first
(left) With a 0–60 (96 km/h) time of 8.2 seconds and a top speed of almost 120 mph (193 km/h), the TR6 needed impact testing to measure its safety levels. Fortunately, the ladder chassis with integral steel body was always regarded as being pretty solid.

LOTUS
ELAN SPRINT

By the time the Elan was released in 1962, motoring devotees knew what to expect from a Lotus. Supreme handling, awesome acceleration, and gorgeous looks were all attributes associated with the Norfolk, England, brand, and the Elan didn't disappoint on any of these counts. Its steel backbone chassis was clothed in a resin-bonded, fiberglass body and the twin-cam 1600cc Ford unit really zipped along. In once again finding a near-perfect balance between speed and handling, Colin Chapman had created a worthy successor to the Lotus Seven *(see pages 104–07)*. The Elan went on to complete five different model series, with the Sprint being its final incarnation. This was also the fastest of the Elans, with a sub-seven-second 0–60 (96 km/h) time and a top speed of 121 mph (195 km/h). Cockpit noise and restricted luggage space aside, the Elan was near faultless, and over 12,000 buyers enjoyed the pleasures of one of the finest enthusiasts' cars of the era.

Fast and racy
In 1964, Peter Sellers announced his engagement to Britt Ekland and his gift to her was a modern take on the "bicycle built for two" – a two-seater Lotus Elan.

Strong bloodline
(right) With a race heritage that included many competition-specific models as well as the Lotus Seven, the Elan was always going to be a favorite with professional and amateur racers.

The exhilarating Elan – race-bred charmer

Lotus owner Colin Chapman designed the Elan as a car for the enthusiast. "Not for the ham-handed or lead-footed," as Lotus promotional material put it, "very definitely for the driver who knows precisely how to handle the most exhilarating sports car in the world." All models in the Elan series were noted for their impressive power and excellent handling. Upgrades to the Ford-based engine brought a steady increase in power through the life of the Elan series, from an at least nominal 105 bhp in 1963 to a genuine 126 bhp in the big-valve engined Sprint. This was a lot of thrust for a lightweight car. A notable byproduct of the Elan series was the Elan Plus 2, introduced in 1967. This was a hardtop with space for two children in the back, allowing the Lotus enthusiast to extend indulgence of his automotive pleasure further into adulthood.

"While not as pretty as the earlier Elite, the Elan definitely had an elfin charm."

Front view

Rear view

Side view

Cabin pressure
Noise levels in the cockpit were high when the top was up.

Design and Production

Model	Lotus Elan Sprint (1970–73)
Production	1,353
Body style	Two-seat drophead.
Construction	Steel box section backbone chassis.
Engine	Four-cylinder twin overhead cam, 1558cc.
Power output	126 bhp at 6500 rpm.
Transmission	Four-speed manual.
Suspension	Independent front and rear.
Brakes	Discs all around.
Max speed	121 mph (195 km/h)

Colin Chapman's genius for auto-engineering gave the Elan a sturdy steel chassis and excellent suspension, while fellow engineer Harry Mundy adapted a Ford Cortina engine to provide the performance to match the handling. Comfort and agility were in large measure due to the "Chapman struts," combined springs and shocks mounted on outriggers at a high angle to the backbone chassis. Abandonment of Lotus's brave experiment with monocoque construction – used for the earlier Elite – put an end to a host of problems. Even though it was aimed at the enthusiast, the sales success of the Elan brought Lotus recognition as a genuine production car manufacturer, even if large numbers were still sold in kit form. By the time the Sprint was in production at the start of the '70s, Lotus had established itself at a new factory in Hethel in Norfolk, England, and was aspiring to move further upmarket.

Engine
(right) The Big-Valve unit developed for the Sprint was claimed to be 25 percent more powerful than the Series 4 block. US models had Stromberg-Zenith carbs rather than Webers.

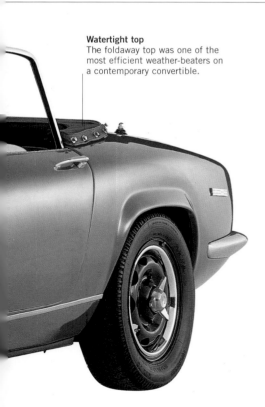

Watertight top
The foldaway top was one of the most efficient weather-beaters on a contemporary convertible.

Motor maestro
(left) Road and Track magazine was full of praise for the Sprint, but debated whether the model's few "imperfections" were simply oversights or down to Colin Chapman not wanting to build a "perfect" sports car that would be of little interest to enthusiasts.

Quality assured
(right) With the Lotus logo in the middle and Chapman's signature engraved on the spoke, drivers felt safe in the knowledge that they would be presented with light, yet assured, steering. And that's exactly what they got.

TRIUMPH
STAG

The Stag could have been such a great car. The look was right, the engine sounded like a Beethoven symphony, there was room for four (just about), and that flush-fitting hardtop and clever roll-over hoop made it both a GT and a convertible. The only serious competition was the contemporary Mercedes SL *(see pages 188–91)*, which was twice the price. But, (and there were so many buts) the Stag was poorly made, unreliable, badly marketed, and consumed engines like popcorn. Excited owners drove their cars away from showrooms only to watch their temperature gauges heading for the red. Soon the secret was out: Triumph's sexy new bolide was a boiler.

The underdeveloped, overhead-cam 3-liter V8 was a disaster, overheating, blowing cylinder head gaskets, ruining crankshafts, and breaking timing chains. After very positive early road tests, the Stag quickly fell from grace and had to be withdrawn from the all-important American market. British Leyland faced huge warranty claims, which, coupled to declining sales, sealed the Stag's fate. Triumph's most promising product was unceremoniously axed in 1977. But the great irony is that if BL had used its splendid Rover 3.5 V8 in the Stag, it would have become a world-class car – it was claimed every engine was needed for the then-new Range Rover, so Triumph had to design its own from scratch. A decision that was supposed to save money, but actually ended up costing millions and destroyed the once-hallowed Triumph brand forever.

Mixed message
(above) Advertising copy played on the fact that while the Stag wasn't cheap, it was "outstanding value for money." A little more contentious was its claim for the "outstanding" engine.

Nice body
The Stag possessed solid, well-designed bodywork and was a real head-turner. Unfortunately, as time went on, it attracted attention on the roads for a different reason – its tendency to break down at every available opportunity.

The deceptive Stag – a mechanical letdown

Triumph promoted the Stag as a Grand Tourer and convertible that could beat the much more expensive Continental models of Mercedes-Benz, Alfa Romeo, and Lancia for sheer style. "Its simple low-lying lines are impeccably cool," crooned the Triumph publicity blurb, "and give it stand-out sophistication among the lumbering herd." Both the driving press and the public were initially struck exactly as Triumph had hoped they would be by the "sporty but suave" look. They were also impressed by the powerplant, a 2997cc V8 with single-overhead-camshaft cylinder heads, delivering 145 bhp for a maximum speed of 120 mph (193 km/h). The gloss soon came off when it turned out that the engine was appallingly unreliable. The fact remains, though, that a Stag in good working order was – and is – a joy to drive, as well as a pleasure to look at.

Front view

Rear view

Side view

Top choice
Buyers could choose between a soft or hardtop.

"The 'no loss' cooling system was no joke for owners who lost their engines to overheating."

Design and Production

Model	Triumph Stag (1970–77)
Production	25,939
Body style	Two-seater convertible.
Construction	Steel body with steel top.
Engine	2997cc V8.
Power output	145 bhp.
Transmission	Four-speed manual with overdrive. Automatic option.
Suspension	Front: independent with coil springs; Rear: independent with coil springs.
Brakes	Front disc, rear drums.
Max speed	120 mph (193 km/h)

The Triumph Stag had its origins in a piece of inspired design by Italian stylist Giovanni Michelotti, the man who had been responsible for the styling of the successful 1963 Triumph 2000 sedan. In 1965, Triumph gave Michelotti an opportunity to indulge himself with the creation of a one-off car show "dream car" based on the 2000. The result was so impressive that the company decided to take it up as the basis for a new four-seater convertible/Grand Tourer. Early prototypes used engines, transmissions, and suspensions from the 2000, but by the time the car finally went into production in 1970 – with bodies made at Triumph's Liverpool factory and assembly in Coventry – it had evolved away from its sedan roots. The Stag was of pressed-steel monocoque construction with coil-spring independent suspension. A new engine was evolved from the unit developed for the Triumph Dolomite. Stag production coincided with a period of especially troubled industrial relations at British Leyland – of which Triumph had been a part since 1961. This no doubt contributed to serious problems with maintaining quality control in the production process.

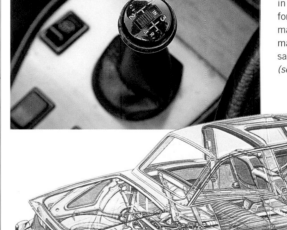

Stubby stick
(left) Transmission was available in either three-speed automatic form or, as here, four-speed manual with overdrive. The manual transmission was the same as that in the TR6 *(see pages 172–75).*

Engine
The Stag's V8 incorporated aluminum alloy cylinder heads and an iron block. The problem with the unit was essentially the cooling system, which wasn't particularly efficient and caused head gaskets to blow. Since production ceased in 1977, many surviving Stags have been equipped with Ford V6 or Rover V8 engines.

Pack your bags
(above) Designed with touring in mind, the Stag had a 14-gallon (63.5-liter) fuel tank and trunk space of 9 ft^3 (.26 m^3).

Rallying cry
(right) "Built to beat the European challenge" may have influenced some, but not the Porsche and Mercedes drivers Triumph was trying to attract.

JAGUAR
E-TYPE V12 ROADSTER

Perfecting perfection can be a doomed endeavor. The V12 E-Type wasn't a bad car, it's just that it could never have been as good as the original E. You see, when Jaguar launched the first E-Type back in '61, everybody agreed (and they still do) that it was automotive perfection at its finest. The way it looked, went, and handled was the closest you could get to the ideal sports car. Which is why trying to improve the unimprovable turned into such a failure. The V12 E of 1971 ballooned in size and weight, got slower and more muted in its responses, lost that lithe purity of line, and shed its magical aura of sexuality. Yes, it was more comfortable, refined, and quiet, the brakes worked and the seats didn't give you a backache. But ask any enthusiast, and they'll tell you that the V12 E was just a pale facsimile of a once brilliant idea.

And, if we're honest, it wasn't that well built either. Unrest at the British Leyland–owned plant in Coventry meant that quality suffered and early cars were plagued with electrical glitches, overheating, and rust. Sales were disappointing, and when the fuel crisis of '74 arrived, the big-drinking V12 E became as popular as Richard Nixon. There was a brief revival of interest in the classic car boom of the Eighties, but these days, everybody wants the gorgeous, uncomplicated beauty of the original E. The portly V12 will always be the poor relation.

Roomier roadster
(above) Known as the Series III, the V12 was essentially a 2+2 roadster, allowing more room for occupants and their luggage than the six-cylinder models.

Lure of the track
(right) V12s competed overseas with some success. Here, Lee Mueller steers his Huffaker Engineering V12 to its first American victory in Seattle, 1974.

Last of the E-Types – more comfort and power

The difference in look between the V12 E-Type and its predecessors was limited but crucial, an accumulation of detail that subtly unmade a design classic. There was a larger air intake, flared arches for the fatter tires, and a longer wheelbase that altered the outline. It was a much heavier car than before, although this was not the fault of the engine; the new bigger unit showed only a small increase in weight over the old XK six. However, enthusiasts might protest, the Series III E-Type was still a handsome car, and a powerful one. Acceleration from 0–60 (96 km/h) in 6.8 seconds was not to be sneezed at. But whereas the 1961 E-Type had gotten away with minor flaws such as poor ventilation because of its exciting image, the more comfort-oriented V12 E could not. Failure to improve such details, plus gas consumption of 16 mpg (5.6 km/l) were the downfall of the last E-Type.

Front view

Rear view

Side view

Air vent

Radiator

Rain protection
Splashguards over the ignition protected against water seepage.

Design and Production

Model	Jaguar E-Type V12 (1971–75)
Production	15,290
Body styles	Two-door, two-seater convertible and coupe.
Construction	Steel monocoque.
Engine	5343cc V12.
Power output	260 bhp.
Transmission	Four-speed manual.
Suspension	Front: independent with torsion bars; Rear: twin coil/spring shock units.
Brakes	Discs all round.
Max speed	150 mph (241 km/h)

It was 1968 when Jaguar announced the existence of a development program to create a new V12 engine. This was originally destined for the XJ6 sedan, and there was some surprise when it surfaced first in the Series III E-Type. Designed by Jaguar engineer Claude Baily, the V12 was originally planned to have two overhead camshafts, but this changed to a more modern and economical single overhead camshaft layout during development.

Although not fundamentally different from earlier series E-Types in construction, the Series III cars all had the longer wheelbase previously used exclusively for 2+2 coupes. The early 1970s were not comfortable years to be part of British Leyland, and quality control in the production of the Series III cars undoubtedly suffered from a demoralized workforce operating amid industrial strife. In all, 15,290 V12s were made – 7,990 of them roadsters.

European superleague
(left) By adding a V12 to the E-Type range, Jaguar joined an elite band of European manufacturers offering the 12-cylinder configuration. And though Jaguar's V12 models never really threatened Ferrari or Maserati, it was due to factors other than the quality of the powerplant.

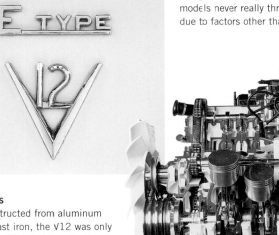

Block stats
(right) Constructed from aluminum alloy and cast iron, the V12 was only about 65 lb (29.5 kg) heavier than the cast-iron XK unit. Four carbs were needed to allow it to breathe.

Hood latch

Lifting the hood
Despite the length of the hood, engine access was good, with the hood raised and held in place by two gas struts. Weight distribution on the V12 was pretty much 50:50, providing a stable ride.

Start of the decline
(left) Even the Series II E-Types, like this one competing in the Transatlantic Race, didn't look brilliant. On the American-spec cars, clumsy license-plate mountings and side markerlights destroyed the purity of line. Open headlights weren't much to look at either.

MERCEDES 280SL

The Mercedes 280SL has mellowed magnificently. In 1963 the new SLs took over the sports mantle of the highly respected, but aging, 190SL *(see pages 80–83)*. Named W113 in Mercedes parlance, they evolved from the original 230SL, through the 250SL, and on to the 280SL, with a more powerful six-cylinder block and higher levels of interior refinements than the 190. The most remarkable thing is how modern they look, for with their uncluttered, clean-shaven looks, it is hard to believe that the last one was made in 1971. Underneath the timelessly elegant sheet metal, they were based closely on earlier Fintail sedans, sharing even the decidedly unsporty recirculating-ball steering.

Yet it is the looks that make this Mercedes something special. The enduring design, with its so-called "pagoda" roof that was higher at the sides than in the middle, was down to Frenchman Paul Bracq. While it may not be the most masculine of models, this well manicured Mercedes is a beautifully built boulevardier that will induce a sense of supreme self satisfaction on any journey.

Still a contender
Always ahead of the game, Mercedes filled the 280SL with features advanced for their time, resulting in a sports car that's still safe and comfortable today.

The sporting SL family
From the 1963 230SL up until the last 500SL models in 1989, Mercedes continually improved its successful line of Sports Light (SL) models.

230SL   280SL   300SL

500SLC

560SL

The admired 280SL – redefining the sports car

Always slated as a "softies" sports car, the Mercedes SL is much more than just a suburban two-seater that feels like a sedan. MB's engineers knew that the bulk of their customers weren't interested in compromise. Fiddly tops, leaking door seals, and wailing engines were not what the average Mercedes buyer expected from the exalted three-pointed-star brand. Hindsight now tells us that most buyers actually want sophistication in a sports car, but Mercedes was the first to realize the fact. And that's why the 280SL was such an important sports car. It set new standards, which meant that roadsters without roofs didn't all have to be damp, drafty, and dismal. Since the 280SL every sports car-maker has held up the Mercedes SL as an iconic benchmark. Many have tried to emulate the concept of the "complete sports car," but none have totally succeeded.

Front view

Rear view

Side view

Engine
Power output gradually increased as the inline sixes grew in size – the 1963 230SL put out 150 bhp, the 1966 250SL managed 160 bhp, and the 2778cc 1968 280SL pushed out 170 horses.

Trademark wipers
Characteristic Mercedes "clap-hands" windshield wipers.

Stopping the 280
The servo-assisted front disc brakes were powerful.

Design and Production

Model	Mercedes 280SL (1968–71)
Production	23,885
Body style	Two-door, two-seat convertible with detachable hardtop.
Construction	Pressed-steel monocoque.
Engine	2778cc inline six, two valves per cylinder, single overhead camshaft.
Power output	170 bhp at 5750 rpm.
Transmission	Four- or five-speed manual, or optional four-speed auto.
Suspension	Front: independent, wishbones, coil springs, telescopic dampers; Rear: swing axle, coil springs, telescopic dampers.
Brakes	Front discs, rear drums.
Max speed	121 mph, auto (195 km/h)

Safe rear
The swing-axle rear suspension was tamed to provide natural understeer.

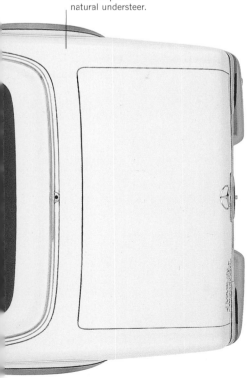

The W113 line started out very like the 190SL *(see pages 80–83)* in character. Beautifully proportioned, exquisitely made, but not in the least bit fast or dynamic. The early 2.3 six-pot engine was pretty slow and the later 2.5 only slightly better. But when Stuttgart dropped its lively 2.8 lump, it suddenly created a very different car and one which was to set the parameters of every Mercedes SL since. The 280SL was now fast and refined. Even coupled to the optional auto box the thing still went exceedingly well. But MB's jewel was now sophisticated too. Gentle tweaking of brakes, suspension, and engine management made the car urgent, poised, and entertaining. A seminal moment in the evolution of the Mercedes Sports, the 280SL went on to spawn the highly successful W107 line of 1971 and laid the footprint for the brilliantly sophisticated W129 500SL of 1990 *(see pages 216–19)*.

Designing a follow-up
(left) The 230, 250, and 280SLs were the original models in the series, but the W113 continued in 1971 when the 280 was replaced by the 350SL. As these sketches show, the 280's delicate lines were replaced by an altogether chunkier, more solid model that was nicknamed *Der Panzerwagen* ("the armored car") by Mercedes engineers.

Interior
(right) The 280 showed its age in its stark interior. The huge steering wheel, painted dash, and abundance of chrome still made it elegant, though. Relatively few were ordered with the manual gearbox, underlining the perception of the SL as more a grand tourer than a genuine sports car.

Ragtop with class
(left) With the addition of a beefier block, the 280SL was no longer considered just a token roadster for well-heeled housewives; it became a more masculine choice, radiating a message of urbane sophistication.

JENSEN-HEALEY
CONVERTIBLE

The Jensen-Healey blew oil, rusted, confused the public, and hastened Jensen's demise. The brainchild of San Francisco car dealer Kjell Qvale, who took over Jensen in the '70s, the Jensen-Healey seemed like a good idea at the time. The West Bromwich, England, firm had just lost its contract to build Austin-Healey bodies and needed another revenue stream. Donald Healey had recently become Jensen's chairman and head of design, so the logic of joining two of Britain's most famous car names on an affordable roadster, which would sell in numbers, seemed irresistible.

But an unreliable Lotus twin-cam engine, alarming propensity for rust, and a world fuel crisis meant the project was doomed from the start. The slab-sided body was slated for looking bland, owners complained of oil leaks and uneven running, the public didn't know if it was a Jensen or a Healey, and, to make matters worse, Jensen's outside component suppliers couldn't get parts to the factory in time. Production peaked at 120 units a week, but then fell sharply as the car's reputation for unreliability hit the press. Various mechanical and cosmetic revisions on the MkII model plus a closed Jensen GT didn't help matters. To survive 1976 Jensen knew it needed $10 (£5) million just to stay afloat, which its bankers refused, so the company was forced to call in the receiver in late '75. Qvale lost $4 (£2) million personally and Birmingham's only carmaker realized too late that the world wasn't yet ready for the big sports car revival.

"The Jensen-Healey project was a viable enough idea, but poor build quality and the energy crisis killed it off."

Vauxhall element
(left) Sitting behind the wheel, it's hard to believe you're riding on a Vauxhall Viva suspension... until you take a corner at high speed.

Late appreciation
Jensen-Healeys may have been criticized at the time, but the model has something of a loyal following today, with numerous enthusiasts' clubs and even a preservation society.

The Jensen-Healey – a tale of unfulfilled expectations

Californian auto trader Kjell Qvale had made a fortune selling Austin-Healey 3000s, Sprites, and MGs. Who could know more than he did about the US market? And who knew more about how to make a winning sports car than Donald Healey? Yet the car they devised and put into production in 1972 failed to press the right buttons with the buying public. In publicity material, the pairing of Jensen and Healey was compared with Rolls and Royce – "a unique fusion of diverse talents, in cars that reflect the best of both." The public did not think so. There was nothing unsatisfactory about the car's performance once reliability problems with the untried Lotus engine were sorted out. Somehow, though, long agonizing over the right look had only achieved an agreeable dullness. Despite improvements such as the new five-speed Getrag transmission in 1974, sales failed to match expectations.

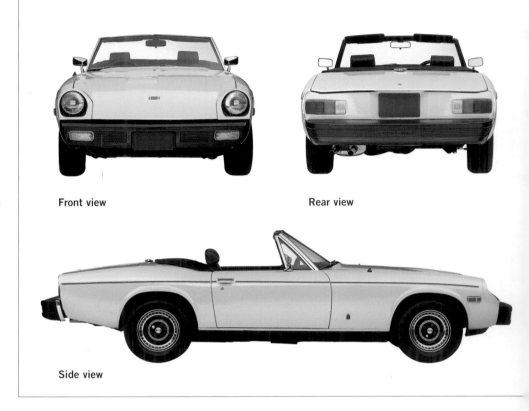

Front view

Rear view

Side view

Engine
The 2-liter Lotus 907 powerplant was one of the first production blocks to incorporate four valves per cylinder. It maxed at over 140 bhp, pushing the Healey to 60 (96 km/h) in 7.8 seconds.

Laminated windshield

Added protection
Bumpers increased in size over the Jensen's lifespan.

Design and Production

Model	Jensen-Healey (1972–76)
Production	10,504
Body styles	Two seater convertible (plus closed Jensen GT).
Construction	Steel monocoque.
Engine	1973cc four-cylinder.
Power output	144 bhp.
Transmission	Four/five speed manual.
Suspension	Front: independent with coil spring; Rear: beam axle with coil spring.
Brakes	Front disc, rear drums.
Max speed	119 mph (192 km/h)

The design of the Jensen-Healey was down to Donald Healey, whose brief from millionaire dealer Kjell Qvale was basically to come up with an MGB-sized sports car that had nothing to do with British Leyland. Healey started out with the intention of using Vauxhall components, but as the project developed, the Vauxhall elements shrunk to just the suspensions and steering gear from the Viva. Eventually, the engine was from Lotus, the four-speed manual transmission from Chrysler, and the pressed-steel unit-construction body/chassis from Jensen. Taking over Jensen and turning it into the production center for their new sports car must have seemed an inspired move to Qvale and Healey in 1970. After all, until recently, Jensen had been making the prestigious Austin-Healey 3000 and Sunbeam Tiger (*see pages 144–47*). But production did not run smoothly and quality control left much to be desired.

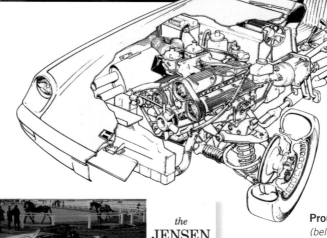

Interior
(*left*) Early cars were a bit basic, with wood trim and carpeting only introduced in 1973.

Paint job
Colour choices included Oakland Green, Sebring Silver, and plain yellow.

Construction
(*above*) The Jensen had a unitized steel body with bolt-on wings. It rode on independent front suspension and a live rear axle.

Proud talk
(*below*) "The making of a classic" is how the sales brochure opened, though history proved otherwise.

the **JENSEN** trio

Top-of-the-range
(*above*) A year or so before folding, Jensen released a luxury-speced GT hardtop to add to its Convertible and Interceptor line-up.

The Sports Car
Revival

"Greed, money, and a culture of instant gratification made sports cars the suburban trinket of the Eighties."

THE RENAISSANCE YEARS

1980

In the Eighties it was politicians rather than politics that changed the fortunes of the sports car. Ronald Reagan gave the American public tax cuts, and Margaret Thatcher told the British that wealth creation was actually a good thing. Sure, the decade didn't start very well – we all remember Triumph's lackluster TR7 – but while British Leyland was pensioning that old clunker , a phalanx of engineers, mostly German, were busily drawing up a completely new sports car order.

By the mid-Eighties Porsche had its 924, 944, 911 *(see pages 200–03)*, and 928. Mercedes' W107 SL was selling faster than ever, and Ferrari's slippery 308 had become an icon. Even cash-strapped Jaguar felt the need to offer an XJS convertible, which while not the best-built Jag ever, certainly looked like a million dollars. And it was money that fueled a new sports car boom. As disposable income soared, demand started tearing away at supply. The market became so bullish that Porsche 911 Turbos, Aston Martin Volantes, and Ferrari Testarossas were able to command unprecedented price premiums.

This was fine if you had epic amounts of cash, but ordinary buyers could only choose ordinary hatchbacks and sedans converted into ragtops. This was the era of the hot-hatchback, when Golf and Escort convertibles were

Timeline 1980–2002

Porsche 911 Carrera 4

• Terrorists seize the Iranian Embassy in London. British SAS personnel storm the building and rescue the 19 hostages. Three of the five gunmen are killed.

• New sports cars include the Porsche 944 16V and Triumph TR7 convertible.

• "Who shot J.R.?" is the question on nearly everyone's minds as the crucial episode of *Dallas* achieves a record of 88.6 million viewers.

• **1981** The DeLorean Gull Wing is launched.

• **1981** IBM introduces the first PC.

• **1982** Maserati launches the Bi-Turbo.

• **1982** Michael Jackson's album *Thriller* is released.

• **1982** The first cellular phone service starts.

• **1984** Joe W. Kittinger makes the first transatlantic balloon flight.

• **1985** Porsche introduces the 944 Turbo.

• **1985** The longest-ever recorded traffic jam, over 40 miles (64 km), forms on the M1 in England after road construction.

• **1985** The European Football Cup Final held at the Heysel stadium in Belgium ends in tragedy as Liverpool and Juventus fans riot. Forty-one spectators are killed.

• **1986** A major nuclear accident occurs at Russia's Chernobyl power station, causing worldwide alarm.

• **1986** The BMW Z-1 model is launched.

• GM buys Lotus.

• A hurricane-force storm in the UK causes immense damage.

• Ferrari launches the F40.

• The "Black Monday" stock market crash causes panic.

Enzo Ferrari

Porsche badge

• Soviet troops retreat from Afghanistan after a nine-year occupation.

• A bomb planted on a Pan Am 747 explodes over Lockerbie, Scotland, killing 270 people.

• Enzo Ferrari dies aged 90.

| 1980 | 1981–83 | 1984–86 | 1987 | 1988 |

the nearest things to the accessible sports car. Only tiny Alfa soldiered on with its Spider, and then only in left-hand drive. But the motormen were quick to spot the market vacuum and started planning the biggest roadster revival since the Sixties. Mazda got there first with its simple and striking MX-5 *(see pages 204–07)*; Mercedes stunned us all with its technically awesome 500SL of '89 *(see pages 216–19)*; and even Lotus rolled out a new Elan.

THE NEW SUPERCARS

As conspicuous consumption became a theology, a cavalcade of high-price supercars arrived on the scene. The Ferrari F40, Jaguar XJ220, Aston Martin Virage,

and Lamborghini Countach became some of the most desirable models in the world, sending out an unequivocal message that fast, flashy cars were back in business, big time. By the early Nineties simply everybody wanted sports cars again, and Rover gave us its MGF, Mercedes the SLK, and Porsche the Boxster. Suburban savings poured into showrooms as retro-styled roadsters became must-have road jewelry. And when the big boys – Ford, GM, Honda, and Toyota – joined the game, it was obvious that the niche sports car wasn't just profitable again, it had evolved into the most desirable and emotional car of them all.

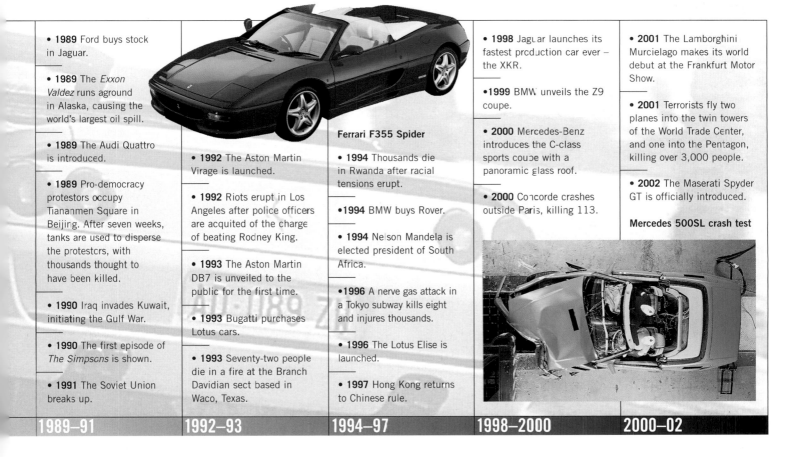

- **1989** Ford buys stock in Jaguar.

- **1989** The *Exxon Valdez* runs aground in Alaska, causing the world's largest oil spill.

- **1989** The Audi Quattro is introduced.

- **1989** Pro-democracy protestors occupy Tiananmen Square in Beijing. After seven weeks, tanks are used to disperse the protestors, with thousands thought to have been killed.

- **1990** Iraq invades Kuwait, initiating the Gulf War.

- **1990** The first episode of *The Simpsons* is shown.

- **1991** The Soviet Union breaks up.

- **1992** The Aston Martin Virage is launched.

- **1992** Riots erupt in Los Angeles after police officers are acquited of the charge of beating Rodney King.

- **1993** The Aston Martin DB7 is unveiled to the public for the first time.

- **1993** Bugatti purchases Lotus cars.

- **1993** Seventy-two people die in a fire at the Branch Davidian sect based in Waco, Texas.

Ferrari F355 Spider

- **1994** Thousands die in Rwanda after racial tensions erupt.

- **1994** BMW buys Rover.

- **1994** Nelson Mandela is elected president of South Africa.

- **1996** A nerve gas attack in a Tokyo subway kills eight and injures thousands.

- **1996** The Lotus Elise is launched.

- **1997** Hong Kong returns to Chinese rule.

- **1998** Jaguar launches its fastest production car ever – the XKR.

- **1999** BMW unveils the Z9 coupe.

- **2000** Mercedes-Benz introduces the C-class sports coupe with a panoramic glass roof.

- **2000** Concorde crashes outside Paris, killing 113.

- **2001** The Lamborghini Murcielago makes its world debut at the Frankfurt Motor Show.

- **2001** Terrorists fly two planes into the twin towers of the World Trade Center, and one into the Pentagon, killing over 3,000 people.

- **2002** The Maserati Spyder GT is officially introduced.

Mercedes 500SL crash test

1989–91   **1992–93**   **1994–97**   **1998–2000**   **2000–02**

PORSCHE 911

If one car could sum up the '80s, it would be the Porsche 911. For close to a decade Porsche's air-cooled screamer became the car to be seen in. Tax cuts and corporate bonuses fired a huge demand, which tore away at a limited supply. Dealers sold every car they could get hold of, and no self-respecting stockbroker would be without his trademark red suspenders and convertible 911.

And, up to a point, you can understand why. Those '87–'89 3.2 Carreras were one of the best 911s of all. They offered a white-knuckle roller-coaster ride, supercar performance, and the real ability to scare you senseless. Get it wrong on the apex of a corner and you'd destroy a small suburb before you stopped spinning. But get it right, and truly understand the 911's handling foibles, and few cars would be able to keep up. In fact many say that those '80s 911s were the last of the real driver's Porsches. These days a well-kept 911 Cabriolet is a neoclassic and one of the most lively and reliable drop-tops money can buy.

Updating a classic
The 911 was given a major redesign in 1998 when it was transformed into a longer, smoother model and given a new 996 designation.

All-time great
For nearly 40 years, 911s have had a reputation for being supremely balanced machines, with top handling and stunning acceleration.

Lovely rear
Though some purists
crit cized the front
restyle of the new
911s, concensus had
it that the designers did
a great job on the rear.

The awesome 911 – still going strong

It's hard to believe the Porsche 911, so often associated with 1980s Yuppies, was originally a product of the early 1960s. It was conceived as a replacement for the aging, VW-based 356 *(see pages 108–11)*. The trademark rear-mounted air-cooled engine was carried over, but this was otherwise an uncompromising all-new design – even if the drooping nose remained as a visible reminder of Beetle origins. The 911 quickly established a reputation as a supremely exhilarating ride for drivers who like to test themselves at the limit of the performance envelope. Although later models became more civilized, the aura of excitement was never entirely lost. The design was to prove amenable to apparently almost limitless development, with increasingly powerful engines mounted in cars marked by repeated evolutions that kept the 911 designation current over four decades.

Front view

Rear view

Side view

Interior
High-spec without being too flashy, the 911's interior is laden with quality features. Automatically adjusting leather seats, a 10-speaker Bose sound system, and heat-insulating glass are just a few of the creature comforts.

Aerodynamic shape
Steeply angled windshield aids low drag coefficient.

Cool wheels
Air dam allows cooling of the wheelarches.

Design and Production

Model	Porsche 911 (1964–2002))
Production	N/A
Body styles	Two-seat convertible coupe, Targa, and Speedster
Construction	Steel monocoque.
Engines	1991cc, 2195cc, 2341cc, 2687cc, 2994cc, 3164cc, 3299cc, 3600cc flat sixes.
Power output	110–430 bhp.
Transmission	Five-speed with automatic and semi-auto options.
Suspension	Front: independent with torsion arms; Rear: independent with torsion arms.
Brakes	Discs all around.
Max speed	124–185 mph (200–298 km/h)

The Porsche flat-six, single-overhead-camshaft air-cooled engine is the core around which the 911 was built. The original 1962 1991cc unit gave 130 bhp, but by the 1980s engines of 3.3 liters and upward were available, with turbocharging for drivers still feeling a little low on power. Four- or five-speed gearboxes, torsion-bar independent suspension front and rear, and four-wheel disc brakes were all used from the outset. The late 1960s and early 1970s brought wider wheels, discreet bumpers to satisfy new safety regulations, and new variants including the 911 Carreras – originally with an engine-lid spoiler – and Targas with removable roof panels. Most people, including Porsche, expected the 911 to gracefully withdraw from the scene in the 1980s, but the cars went from strength to strength. The 1989 four-wheel drive Carrera 4 represented a notable degree of innovation. By then hundreds of thousands of 911s had been sold, with no end in sight to the course of their evolution.

Boxster similarities
(right) As well as the same range of colors on offer, the new 911 shared more manifest features with its Boxster stablemate, including the headlights and much of the interior fixtures.

Lightweight alloys
18-in (46-cm), five-spoke alloy wheel.

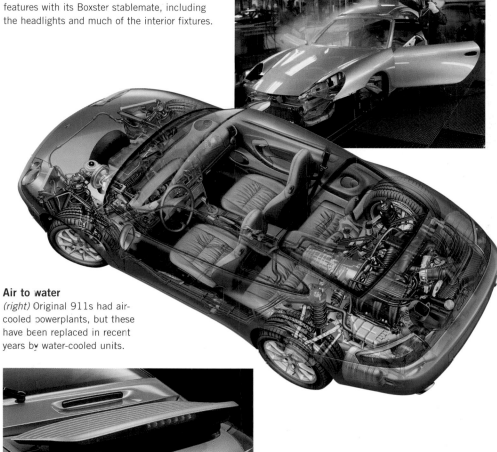

Air to water
(right) Original 911s had air-cooled powerplants, but these have been replaced in recent years by water-cooled units.

Back down
(left) The rear spoiler reduces tail-end lift at high speeds and used to be attached to the 911's rear. Recent models sport electronic versions that can be raised at the flick of a switch.

A joy to drive
The MX-5 has always been an effortless drive, its low center of gravity, well-engineered chassis, and almost perfect weight distribution contributing to fantastic roadholding abilities.

First revison
After nine years in production with a model that, visually at least, remained essentially unchanged, Mazda relaunched the MX-5 in 1998 with an all-new body. Proportions were pretty much the same, but the pop-up headlights gave way to faired-in examples.

MAZDA MX-5

"The MX-5 is rightly considered one of the few genuine enthusiasts' cars of the late 20th century."

The MX-5 single-handedly kick-started the world's long-dormant sports car market. A Japanese copy of the British Lotus Elan *(see pages 176–79)* of the Sixties, Mazda's most successful roadster was that unique thing: a sports car you didn't have to suffer to own. Endlessly reliable, uncomplicated, and cheap to run, it debuted at the 1989 Chicago Auto Show to rapturous applause. Everyone asked how a Japanese car company (usually known for the automotive equivalent of fast food) could produce something that felt so sweet, refined, nimble, and essentially "right"? Critics also wondered how traditionally fussy Japanese car designers had managed to pen such a classically simple and elegant silhouette?

By designing it in California, that's how. The MX-5 was shaped in Mazda's Los Angeles studio, and its near-perfect demeanor was the result of canvassing thousands of Americans on exactly what they wanted from a sports car. Even the exhaust note was determined by customer clinics. A shrewd strategy, because when prototypes emerged from the styling studio, they were pursued by scores of joggers waving checkbooks, desperate to place orders. The rest, as they say, is history, and Mazda's roadster can claim to have been one of the most influential cars of its decade and responsible for the likes of Mercedes' SLK, Porsche's Boxster, the MGF, and Fiat's Barchetta. Without the MX-5, the world's motor industry would never have bothered reinventing the sports car, and the Nineties would be remembered as just another era of dull and dreary sedans.

The cute MX-5 – retro but modern

Marketing the MX-5, Mazda described its aim as "to produce a sports car that embodied the traditional spirit of the two-seater roadster of old." You would feel the exhilaration of the wind in your hair, but without the drawbacks that had forced the much-loved MGs and Triumphs out of the marketplace. Mazda designers and market researchers spent four years working to carry off this exercise successfully. Styling was not too much of a problem, since there were plenty of old British sports cars to use as models. Achieving the nostalgic look and nimble handling without offending against modern expectations of safety, comfort, and reliability was much more difficult. A harsh exhaust note deliberately cultivated for effect, rather than an unavoidable byproduct of the engineering, was a masterly move. In the end, the MX-5 was fun but practical, retro but entirely modern.

Front view

Rear view

Side view

Tough top

Extra shift
Latest models have a six-speed transmission.

Five-spoke alloy wheel

Design and Production

Model	Mazda MX-5 (1989–)
Production	N/A
Body style	Two-seater convertible with optional hardtop.
Construction	Steel monocoque.
Engines	1598cc and 1839cc four cylinder.
Power output	114–146 bhp.
Transmission	Five- or six-speed manual.
Suspension	Front and rear independent with coil springs.
Brakes	Discs all around.
Max speed	115 mph (185 km/h)

One of the lessons Mazda designers learned from the classic sports models was to keep down weight. The monocoque body-cum-chassis had to be a strong structure to give the degree of safety required today, but the use of high-tensile steel made it relatively light, while giving more than satisfactory rigidity. Lightweight materials were used wherever possible, as in the hood and bumpers. There was an aluminum subframe and an aluminium head for the engine. With the car weighing in at 2,106 lb (955 kg), the 114 bhp delivered by the four-cylinder electronic-fuel-injection 1598cc engine was more than adequate for an exciting drive. There was power-assisted rack-and-pinion steering, a short gearshift for race-car style shifts, four-wheel discs, and finely-calibrated springs and shock-absorbers designed to give maximum comfort – no shake, rattle, and roll for this roadster. Upgrading brought inevitable changes over the first decade of the MX-5's existence. By 1999, the engine was delivering 140 bhp and there were novel features such as variable intake control for the air intakes. But the car was still right for the price and looked like it would sell well on into the new millennium.

Firm underpinnings
(right) The all-steel monocoque body was designed to be strong but light. Through the '90s Mazda added braces and stiffeners to provide extra rigidity.

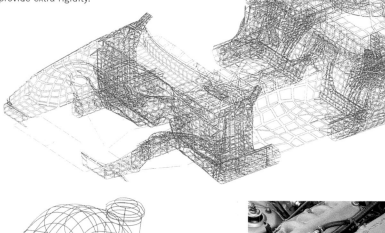

Rear electrics
Early MX-5s had the battery in the trunk.

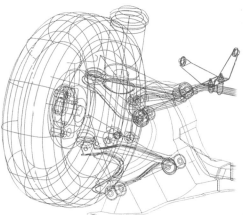

Riding the bumps
(above) The unequal length, double-wishbone suspension was specially-developed by Mazda to allow maximum contact with the road. It has proved to be effective enough – it is still in use today.

Reliable unit
(above) Original displacement on the 16-valve, dohc was 1598cc. An 1839cc block was offered soon after, and it remains at the core of the current MX-5 range, though fuel injection and sequential valve timing allow the latest models to output 146 bhp.

FERRARI
F355 SPIDER

The Ferrari F355 is one of the best driving cars ever. Ask anybody who's owned one. The wonderfully urgent 3.5 V8 will scream all the way to 8,500 rpm, which in sixth gear equates to a mighty 185 mph (298 km/h), maybe a touch more if you're brave enough to edge it past the red line. The steering is scalpel sharp, the brakes hugely powerful, and the balance and poise of the suspension unbelievable. Look underneath, and you'll see that the floorpan is completely flat. All the usual pipes and wiring are hidden under a smooth panel to help the 355 cleave the air like a missile. Which it does with awesome dispatch.

And it's also reliable. Ferraris of the '70s and '80s were as well built as an Austin Allegro, but in the '90s the prancing horse gained a new engineering integrity. 355s are dependable enough to be used every day and are one of Ferrari's all-time great machines. This is automotive pornography at its very finest.

Added protection
Double-thickness sheet steel bodywork ensures that this stupendously fast car is also a safe one.

Space "issue"
There may only be room for a mobile phone in the 355's trunk, but frankly, who cares?

"Don't be fooled by the 355's compact dimensions and pretty looks – this is a formidably fast car."

High esteem
The stunning looks, glorious engine, incredible handling, and very special way in which the F355 communicates with the driver has made it one of Moderna's most admired and successful products.

The luscious Spider – a true return to form

Powerful as it is, the F355 Spider ranks as one of the smaller mid-engined Ferraris. It was launched in 1994 to replace the largely unloved F348 in this category, and did so in style, establishing clear superiority over its predecessor in power, handling, and looks. Mounted sideways behind the seats, the V8 engine gave acceleration from 0–60 (96 km/h) in 4.6 seconds – impressive by any standards. The styling was, almost inevitably, the product of Ferrari's favorite design bureau, Pininfarina. According to Ferrari, some 1,800 hours of wind-tunnel tests went into making the body shape as aerodynamically efficient as possible, with a lot of careful thought given not just to reducing drag but to increasing down-forces for grip. The Pininfarina touch also made sure that the car would be an object of sheer beauty – clean, perfectly proportioned, and discreetly curvaceous.

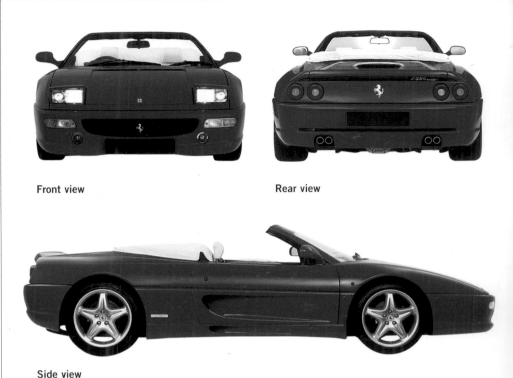

Front view

Rear view

Side view

Automatic top
The hood was raised by an electronic system.

Mid-engined
The engine was positioned behind the seats.

Design and Production

Model	Ferrari F355 (1995–99)
Production	N/A
Body styles	Two seater convertible, coupe, and targa.
Construction	Steel and alloy monocoque.
Engine	3496cc V8.
Power output	380 bhp.
Transmission	Six-speed manual.
Suspension	Front: independent with coil springs; Rear: independent with coil springs.
Brakes	Discs all around.
Max speed	185 mph (298 km/h)

Until the death of the patriarchal Enzo Ferrari in 1988, Ferrari had remained in essence a family firm, despite being taken over by Fiat. The factory at Maranello was never committed to production on the scale of, for example, Porsche, nor could it match the quality of German engineering. But by the 1990s, Fiat was firmly in control and, whether by coincidence or not, engineering standards at Maranello shook off a reputation for second-rateness. The F355 is high on quality and innovation. The rear-mounted engine, a 90-degree 3496cc V8, delivers 380 bhp. The sheet metal monocoque body and chassis is light but rigid, attached to the tubular subframe, engine, and suspension by laser welding. The front and rear suspensions feature unequal length wishbones. A sophisticated shock absorber system is fed information from sensors about the movement of the car and adjusts accordingly. The shocks also have two settings for the driver to select – sport or comfort – for a more or less exciting drive. Rack-and-pinion power-assisted steering, a six-speed gearbox, disc brakes – what is there left to desire?

Luggage space

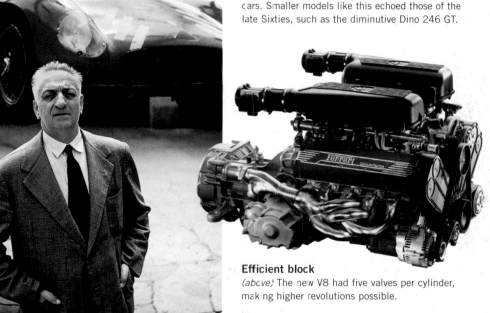

Enzo's ethos
(left) The F355 continued Enzo Ferrari's ideal of making beautifully crafted, well-engineered sports cars. Smaller models like this echoed those of the late Sixties, such as the diminutive Dino 246 GT.

Efficient block
(above) The new V8 had five valves per cylinder, making higher revolutions possible.

Thorough testing
(right) Ferrari's aerodynamicists were meticulous in testing the prototype's design. The floorplan shape was constructed in a way that maximized aerodynamic efficiency without relying on specific ground clearance.

TVR GRIFFITH

Griffith 500

Reincarnations are rarely successful. And when car companies dust off an old name and bolt it to a new product, there's always some compromise. But not the TVR Griffith. The original '60s version was frighteningly fast, with a Cobra engine *(see pages 148–51)* and a sub-five-second 60 (96 km/h) time. But the '90s Griffith isn't just quick, it's infinitely more entertaining. Hand-made in the seaside town of Blackpool, the modern Griffith boasts a 4.3-litre Rover V8, carbon-fiber panels, and a sumptuous leather-lined cabin. Slick touches abound like transmission tunnel-mounted door latches and a spun-alloy gear knob.

Yes, the Griffith is pretty, and it's shrewdly designed, but its greatest attribute, like its namesake, is its utterly stupefying performance. Top tilt is 161 mph (259 km/h) and 60 mph (96 km/h) comes up in a breathless 4.7 seconds, accompanied by one of the best V8 soundtracks you'll hear in the modern world.

Nostalgia revived
The response when the accelerator is depressed harks back to an earlier era of classic British sports cars.

Safe at high speed
All hell breaks loose when the Griffith's wall of torque kicks in, but the finely balanced chassis keeps you on track.

Supremely engineered
Faster than many supercars more than three times
its price, there's no questioning the Griffith's
credentials as a genuine sports thoroughbred.

"You don't buy TVRs because they're endlessly reliable, but
because they give you those unique and very special golden
moments that no other car can."

The stylish Griffith – pure British grunt

The Griffith 4.3 caused a sensation when first unveiled in 1990 – some compared its impact to the Jaguar E-Type in 1961 *(see pages 124–27)*. The smooth sweep of the swaggeringly curvaceous carbon-fiber body was not interrupted by anything as banal as a door handle or a latch for the trunk, while the souped-up Rover V8 promised major-league performance. Success was confirmed after deliveries to customers began in 1992, even if steering that required some muscle at times made this a car for real drivers only. Originally on sale for $41,000 (£27,000), it was close to being the sale of the century. Quicker to 120 mph (193 km/h) than either a Porsche 911 *(see pages 200–03)* or a Ferrari Testarossa, it cost a third or a quarter of their price. Followed up with cars such as the Chimaera and the Cerbera, the Griffith established TVR's place among the front rank of world sports car manufacturers.

Front view

Rear view

Side view

Inside hide
Half-leather interior came as standard.

Fair size
Chunky boot offered reasonable luggage space.

Design and Production

Model	TVR Griffith (1991–2002)
Production	N/A
Body style	Two-seat convertible.
Construction	Steel chassis, GRP body.
Engines	3948cc, 4280cc, 4988cc V8s.
Power output	240–340 bhp.
Transmission	Five-speed manual.
Suspension	Front: independent with coil springs; Rear: independent with coil springs.
Brakes	Discs all around.
Max speed	158–165 mph (254–266 km/h)

Blackpool, England-based firm TVR set the formula for its cheap-for-what-you-get sports cars back in the 1950s with models such as the Grantura – make a stylish fiberglass body, fit it to a strong tubular-steel chassis, and put a powerful bought-in engine under the hood to give surprisingly impressive performance. For a long time selling most of its cars in kit form, under new owner Peter Wheeler in the 1980s TVR repositioned itself as a provider of altogether plusher finished articles, still hoping to undercut the famous supercar manufacturers on price while matching them on style and performance. For the 1990s Griffith, a carbon-fiber body was allied to a chassis based on that used in the 1980s TVR S-series cars. A 3.9-liter Rover V8 engine was radically worked over by TVR's Coventry-based sister company TVR Power to create a 4.3-liter unit delivering 280 bhp at 5500 rpm and impressive torque to match. Largely as a result of the success of the Griffith, TVR has become a maker of cars in thousands rather than in hundreds.

Muscular flanks
(right) With its bulbous doors, seven-spoke alloys, and E-Type-esque headlights, the Griffith was a distinctive presence on the road.

Fast blocks
All engines offered a sub-five-second 0–60 (96 km/h) time.

— **Faired-in headlight**

Interior
(left) The genuine walnut dash was stylishly peppered with retro dials, the alloy gearstick knob enhancing the air of performance luxury. An adjustable steering wheel and supportive seats provided essential comfort backup.

Tried and tested
(right) As with most TVRs, the Griffith had a glass-reinforced plastic bodyshell that slipped over a space-frame chassis. It was a great combination, and needed to be to ensure that the 300-plus horses were kept in line.

MERCEDES
500SL

For 10 years, the 500SL was the most refined and technically-audacious sports car in the world. An engineering *tour de force*, Mercedes' most sophisticated offering boasted a power-top, electronic antiskid braking, gas suspension, aluminum hardtop, automatic roll bar that raised itself in 0.3 of a second, 32-valve V8 engine, plus anti-dive and anti-squat control. In fact, the 500SL's preeminence as the finest sports car money could buy was only eclipsed by the new SL of 2001. Road testers in the Nineties raved about the beauty of the 500's construction, silence, safety, performance, and unflappable road manners. And with its ultralight, flush-fitting hardtop or power top that could be raised or lowered in less than 30 seconds, it could be both snug coupe or open roadster.

Despite costing the price of a small house, the 500 sold well throughout its 10-year run, spawning engine options of 2.8, 3.0, 3.2, and even a 6.0 V12. Bought by tycoons and media celebrities, many were equipped with AMG performance options and given alloy wheels and impressively wide tires. Classy, restrained, and very opulent, the 500 became a regular sight wherever large amounts of money came to rest. But the greatest validation of the 500's depth of engineering is that after 10 years and 100,000 hard miles (161,000 kilometers), all those electric motors, relays, control units, and sensors usually work as perfectly as the day they were assembled.

Dynamic Mercedes
The 500SL cuts a mean image in the rear-view mirror, capturing the Mercedes ethos of refined design and supreme engineering.

All-around excellence
A top speed of 155 mph (250 km/h) was possible on the autobahns, but you could happily throw this classy car around winding back roads with no problems at all.

"In the history of the automobile, very few cars have attracted the level of acclaim given to the 500SL."

The peerless 500SL – setting new standards in sports luxury

The Mercedes 500SL was a car that gave you luxuries you never knew you wanted – seats that heat up in cold weather and adjust in every direction through five separate electric motors, and a front end designed to scoop up any unfortunate pedestrian you might hit and roll them over the hood. And luxuries you always knew you wanted, but thought you would never have, like a top that could be raised or lowered in seconds at the touch of a button. The car had the kind of simple, classic good looks generally referred to as "timeless" – without quirkiness or gimmickry. Some might complain that the luxury lightness of the power-assisted steering and the electronic feedback devices designed to stop you from screwing up took the fun out of the driving. But then driving the 500SL was not meant to be fun – it was serious pleasure.

Front view

Rear view

Side view

Svelte design
The closed soft top sat almost flush to the bodywork.

Rear seat belt slot

Fuel cap
Fuel consumption of 18 mpg (6.3 km/l) was no surprise on a 5-liter V8.

Design and Production

Model	Mercedes 500SL (1989–2001)
Production	N/A
Body style	Two-seat sports convertible.
Construction	Steel body, aluminum hardtop.
Engine	4973cc V8.
Power output	326 bhp.
Transmission	Four-speed automatic.
Suspension	Front: independent with anti-dive anti-squat; Rear: independent.
Brakes	Discs all around.
Max speed	155 mph (250 km/h)

Development of the 500SL took eight years, from 1981 to 1989. Bruno Sacco and his Mercedes design team put a huge amount of wind-tunnel and computer work into the shape of the car, which improved significantly in aerodynamics through the development process. Part of their brief was to make the car ultrasafe, which produced features such as the strong bodyshell, the self-raising roll bar, and the cast-metal seats integrated into the body structure. Concern for structural strength and the host of electronic servomotors and gizmos meant this was never going to be a lightweight car and it needed a lot of power. Which of course it got. Bottom-of-the line models had variants on the Mercedes inline six, while pricier V8 and eventually V12 options were available. Despite the complexity of electronics such as the Bosch engine management system, the 500SL never revealed even a hint of unreliability.

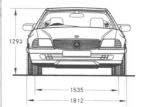
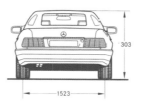

Solid sportster

(left) At 17¾ ft (4.5 m) in length and 7 ft (1.81 m) wide, the 500SL wasn't exactly petite, but few sports models have ever been as imposing in their design. The price to pay for its wealth of electronic gadgetry and unparalleled safety features was a curbside weight of 4,010 lb (1,918 kg).

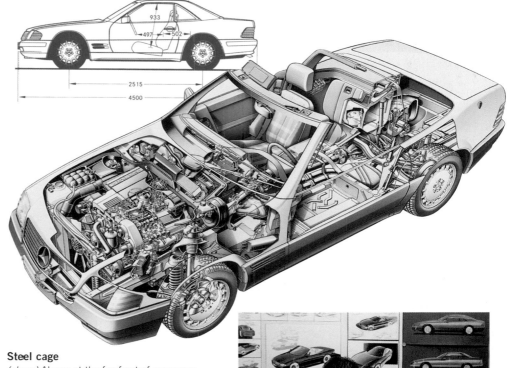

Steel cage

(above) Always at the forefront of passenger protection, Mercedes created an incredibly strong bodyshell for the 500, and made elements such as the headrests integral to the structure.

From the drawing board

(right) The 500SL's design was constantly refined using computers, wind tunnels, and good old-fashioned line drawings.

INDEX

A

AC
    428 156–59
    Ace Bristol 88–91
    Aceca 91
    Cobra 427 148–51
    Shelby American Cobra 151
Aero 8, Morgan 170
Alfa Romeo
    Duetto Spider 164
    Giulietta Spider 72–75
    Junior 1300 Spider 164–67
    Super Spider 75
    Veloce Spider 75
Alpine, Sunbeam 96–99
Appleyard, Ian 29
Arkus-Duntov, Zora 62
Aston Martin DB3S 40–43
Aurelia B24 Spider, Lancia 64–67
Austin-Healey
    100 116, 117
    3000 116–19
    Big Healey 116–19
    Bugeye 92
    Frogeye Sprite MkI 12, 92–95

B

Baily, Claude
    Jaguar E-Type V12 Roadster 187
    Jaguar XK120 31
Bentley, W.O. 42
Bertone styling 75
Big Healey, Austin-Healey 116–19
Bindurant, Bob 152
Bira, Prince 34
Black, Sir John 174
BMW
    3 Series 7, 12
    328 9, 18, 32–35
    507 84–87
Boyer, Bill 71
Bracq, Paul 188
Bristol, AC Ace- 88–91
Brooks, Tony 43
Brown, David 42
Bugeye, Austin-Healey 92–93

C

C-Type, Jaguar 9, 48–51
Carrera, Porsche 911 110
Cat *see* Jaguar
Caterham Seven 104

[no heading]

Chapman, Colin
    Lotus Elan Sprint 13, 176, 178, 179
    Lotus Seven 104–07
Chapman, W.R. 25
Chevrolet
    Corvette 60–63
    Corvette Sting Ray 136–39
    EX-122 60
Cobb, John 19
Cobra
    AC 427 148–51
    link with Ford 151
Coker, Gerry 95
Cole, Ed 62
Cooper, Mini 7
Corvette, Chevrolet 60–63
Corvette Sting Ray, Chevrolet 136–39
Crompton, Geoff 99

D

D-Type, Jaguar 9, 44, 48
Daimler SP250 Dart 112–15
Daninos, Jean 120, 122
Dart, Daimler SP250 112–15
Datsun Fairlady 1600 152–55
d'Oliviera, Casmiro 22
Duetto Spider, Alfa Romeo 164

E

E-Type
    Jaguar 124–27
    V12 Roadster, Jaguar 184–87
Earl, Harley 60, 115
Eberhorst, Eberan von 43
Elan Sprint, Lotus 176–79

F

Facel Vega Facellia 120–23
Fairlady 1600, Datsun 152–55
Fangio, Juan 142
Feidler, Fritz 35
Ferrari F355 Spider 208–11
Ford
    Cobra 151
    Thunderbird 60–61, 68–71
Frogeye Sprite MkI, Austin-Healey 92–95
Frua, Pietro
    AC428 156, 158, 159
    Maserati Mistrale Spyder 140, 143

G

Giulietta Spider, Alfa Romeo 72–75
Goertz, Albrecht 84, 86, 87
Grantura, TVR 215
Griffith, TVR 212–15

H

Hamilton, Duncan 44, 50, 51
Hassan, Walter 31
Healey, Donald
    Austin-Healey 3000 116
    Jensen-Healey Convertible 192, 194, 195
Henna, Ernest 34
Heynes, Bill
    Jaguar SS100 23
    Jaguar XK120 31
Hoffman, Max
    Alfa Romeo Giulietta Spider 67
    BMW 507 87
Hopkirk, Paddy 119
Howes, Kenneth 99

I J

Iizuka, Hidehiro 155
Jaguar
    C-Type 9, 48–51
    D-Type 9, 44, 48
    E-Type 10, 102, 124–27
    V12 Roadster 184–87
    Series III 185
    SS90 23
    SS100 20–23
    Super Sports 28
    XK120 19, 28–31
    XKE 124
    XKSS 44–47
    see also Daimler
Jano, Vittorio 67
Jensen Motors and Sunbeam Tiger 147
Jensen-Healey Convertible 192–95

K

Karmann design 172, 175
Kimber, Cecil 27
Kommeda, Irwin 109

L

Lancia
    Aurelia B24 Spider 64–67
    B20 GT Coupé 64
    Super Spider 67
Lord, Leonard 94, 116
Lotus
    Elan Sprint 176–79
    Seven 104–07
Lyons, William
    Daimler SP250 Dart 113
    Jaguar C-Type 48
    Jaguar XK120 31
    Jaguar XKSS 44, 46

M

McCann, B.C. 67
Makinen, Timo 119
Marchetti, Carlo 123

Maserati
    Mistrale Spyder 140–43
    Sebring 143
    Tipo 109 140–43
Mazda, MX-5 204–07
Mercedes
    190SL 80–83
    280SL 188–91
    300SL 39, 83
    500SL 216–19
    W113 188–91
MG
    A 76–79
    B 132–35
    EX182 76
    TB 24
    TC Midget 18, 24–27
    TD 27
    TF 27, 79
Michelotti, Giovanni
    Triumph Spitfire Mk3 129, 131
    Triumph Stag 183
    Triumph TR6 175
Midget, MG TC 24–27
Miles, Ken 145
Mistrale Spyder, Maserati 140–43
Mitchell, Bill 136
Morgan
    Aero 8 170
    Plus Eight 168–71
    Plus Four 52–55
Moss, Stirling
    Aston Martin DB3S 43

Austin-Healey Frogeye Sprite 93, 94
Jaguar C-Type 49, 50
Maserati Mistrale Spyder 142
Mueller, Lee 185
Mundy, Harry 179

O P

Orsi, Omer 142
Parkinson, Dan 153
Parnell, Reg 43
Pininfarina, Battista
 Alfa Romeo 1300 167
 Alfa Romeo Giulietta Spider 72, 75
 Ferrari F355 Spider 210
 Lancia Aurelia B24 Spider 67
Plus Eight, Morgan 168–71
Plus Four, Morgan 52–55
Porsche
 356B 38–39, 108–11
 911 200–03
 Carrera 110, 203
 Targa 203

Q R

Qvale, Kjell 192, 194, 195
Richardson, Ken 57, 58
Roadster, Jaguar E-Type V12 184–7
Rolt, Tony 50, 51

S

Salvadori, Roy 43
Sayer, Malcolm

Jaguar C-Type 51
Jaguar E-Type 126, 127
Jaguar XKSS 46
Seaman, Dick 34
Sebring, Maserati 143
Shelby American Cobra 151
Shelby, Carroll
 AC Cobra 427 148, 150, 151
 Aston Martin DB3S 43
 Sunbeam Tiger 145, 147
Spider
 Alfa Romeo
  Duetto 164
  Giulietta 72–75
  Junior 1300 164–67
  Super 75
  Veloce 75
 Ferrari F355 208–11
 Lancia
  Aurelia B24 64–67
  Super 67
Spitfire MK3, Triumph 128–31
sports car
 definition of 6–8
 motorsports 8–11
 racing connections 8–11
 renaissance 13–14, 198–99
 saloon 11–13
Sports, Triumph 56
Sprint, Lotus Elan 176–79
Sprite MkI, Austin-Healey Frogeye 92–95
Spyder, Maserati Mistrale 140–43
Stag, Triumph 180–83

Sting Ray, Chevrolet Corvette 136–39
Sunbeam
 Alpine 96–99
 Tiger 144–47

T

Targa, Porsche 203
Thunderbird, Ford 60–61, 68–71
Tiger, Sunbeam 144–47
Tipo 109, Maserati 140–43
Tojeiro, John 88, 91
Triumph
 20TS 59
 Spitfire MK3 128–31
 Sports 56
 Stag 180–83
 TR1 59
 TR2 56–59
 TR6 172–75
 TR7 13, 172
 TRX 59
Turner, Edward 114, 115
TVR
 Grantura 215
 Griffith 212–15

V

Veloce Spider, Alfa Romeo 75
'Vette see Chevrolet Corvette
Virgilio, Francesco de 67

W Z

Walker, Peter 50
Wallwork, Johnny 58
Watson, Willie 41
Weslake, Harry 23
Wharton, Ken 76
Wheeler, Peter 215
Whitehead, Peter 50
Wintersteen, George 136
Wisdom, Tommy 22
Zaccone-Mina, Ettore 67

ACKNOWLEDGMENTS

The author would like to thank Phil Hunt for his tireless efforts in putting this book together.

Dorling Kindersley would like to thank the following for their contributions: Reg Grant and Hazel Richardson for additional text; Derek Coombes, Simon Wilder, and Dawn Young for design assistance; Karen Constanti for DTP assistance; Cynthia Frazer and Anna Bedewell for picture research; David Saldanha for picture library research; Beth Apple for jacket text; Chris Drew and Natalie Godwin for jacket design; Margaret McCormack for the index; James Mann, Matthew Ward, Michael Labat, Luke Parminter, George Solomonides, and Andrew Dee for photography; Pooks Motor Book Shop; and Soph Moeng of Midsummer Books.

Dorling Kindersley would also like to thank the following for allowing their cars to be photographed: David Stoodley's Red Daimler Dart, Steve Trotman's E-Type FHC 1968 Series III, Ken Parsons' E-Type Series III Roadster, Brian Marshell's 1964 E-Type Roadster, Graham Phillips' MGA, Tony Hayes' MGB, Ken Connolly's MG TC, Robert Ingham's MG TF, David Massey's MGB, John Kent's Austin-Healey 3000, Chris Dimmock's Austin-Healey 3000, Bert and Gwen Langford's 1959 MkI AH Frogeye Sprite, Robert and Anne Kai's Mazda MX-5, Maurice Blackwood's Lotus Seven, Anne Blackwood's Lotus Elan, Keith Manning's Triumph TR2, Peter Ward's TR6, Lawrie and Kaye Placin's Stag, Rod Wilkes' Spitfire, Lindsay Burke's MX-5, Steve Trotman's E-Type FHC 1969 Series II, Peter Matthews' Sunbeam Alpine, Richard Heading's Jensen-Healey, Angus McLeod's 1961 Alfa Romeo Giulietta, Darryl Brooksbank's Facel Vega, John Tudor's Jaguar E-Type Roadster, Roger Lucas' Maserati Mistrale Spyder, Simon Ridge's Alpha Giulietta Spider, Peter Coombes' Alfa Giulietta Spider, Anthony Hussey's Aurelia Spider, Simon Bathhurst Brown's AC Ace, Michael Trotter's AC428, Roger Edwards' Mercedes 280SL, Bill Maycock's Mercedes 500SL, Tristan Bradfield's Sunbeam Tiger, Tom Falconer's Corvette, Achim Gloger's Morgan Plus Eight, Martyn Apsey's TVR Griffith, and Richard Pooley's Morgan Plus Four.

Photography Credits:
James Mann: pp 2–3, 6, 24-25, 48-49, 52-53, 56-57, 64-65, 72-73, 76-77, 88-89, 92-93, 96-97, 104-105, 112-113, 116-117, 120-121, 124-125, 128-129, 132-133, 136-137, 144-145, 148-149, 156-157, 168-169, 172-173, 176-177, 180-181, 184-185, 188-189, 192-193, 204-205, 212-213, 216-217
Matthew Ward: pp 142-143, 186-187

Picture Credits:
The position of the pictures is indicated as follows: t=top, b=bottom, r=right, l=left, c=center
pp 1: Motoring Picture Library/National Motor Museum (bl), Porsche Ag (br); **5:** Neill Bruce Motoring Photolibrary (bl), GP Library (br); **6:** BMIHT, Magna Press (tl); **7:** BMW AG Historical Archive (b); **8:** BMW AG Historical Archive (b); **9:** Advertising Archives (tr), Ludvigsen Library (br); **10:** GP Library (b); **11:** Jaguar Daimler Heritage Trust (tr), Motoring Picture Library/National Motor Museum (b); **12:** Motoring Picture Library/National Motor Museum (bl); **13:** Ludvigsen Library (bl); **14:** Motoring Picture Library/National Motor Museum (tl); **15:** Porsche Ag; **17:** Auto Express (br), BMW AG Historical Archive (bc); **18:** British Motor Industry Heritage Trust (br), Neill Bruce Motoring Photolibrary (bl); Peter Roberts Collection (cr); **18–19:** GP Library; **19:** BMW AG Historical Archive (cr); **20:** Neill Bruce Motoring Photolibrary, Peter Roberts Collection (br); **20–21:** Jaguar Daimler Heritage Trust; **23:** British Motor Industry Heritage Trust (tcr); **25:** Motoring Picture Library/National Motor Museum (br); **27:** Neill Bruce Motoring Photolibrary (tc), Peter Roberts Collection (c), GP Library (bc); **28–29:** Neill Bruce Motoring Photolibrary, Peter Roberts Collection; **29:** Ronald Grant Archive: From *Island in the Sun*/Twentieth Century Fox (tr), Motoring Picture Library/National Motor Museum (tc); **31:** Jaguar Daimler Heritage Trust (cr), Motoring Picture Library/National Motor Museum (tcl); **32:** BMW AG Historical Archive (tc), James Mann (tr); **32–33:** Motoring Picture Library/National Motor Museum; **33:** BMW AG Historical Archive (tl); **35:** BMW AG Historical Archive (c) (cr) (bc); **37:** BMW AG Historical Archive (br), Motoring Picture Library/National Motor Museum (bc); **38:** Neill Bruce Motoring Photolibrary, Peter Roberts Collection (cr); **38–39:** GP Library; **39:** Motoring Picture Library/National Motor Museum (br); **40:** Lat Photographic (bc), Roger Stowers (br); **40–41:** GP Library; **41:** Lat Photographic (bc), Roger Stowers (bl) (br); **43:** Neill Bruce Motoring Photolibrary, Peter Roberts Collection(bc); **44:** Neill Bruce Motoring Photolibrary (bl); **44–45:** Jaguar Daimler Heritage Trust; **47:** Neill Bruce Motoring Photolibrary (tl), Jaguar Daimler Heritage Trust (crb);

48–49: Motoring Picture Library/National Motor Museum; 49: Neill Bruce Motoring Photolibrary, Peter Roberts Collection (tc) (tr), Ludvigsen Library (tl); 51: Jaguar Daimler Heritage Trust (tcr) (crb) (br), James Mann (c); 52: Morgan Motor Company (bl) (bc); 55: Morgan Motor Company (cr) (bc); 56: Neill Bruce Motoring Photolibrary, Peter Roberts Collection (tr); 59: Motoring Picture Library/National Motor Museum (tcl); 60: Lat Photographic (bl), Motoring Picture Library/National Motor Museum (bc), Neill Bruce Motoring Photolibrary (br); 60–61: 1993 Cindy Lewis; 61: Lat Photographic (bl) (bc); 63: Neill Bruce Motoring Photolibrary, Peter Roberts Collection (cr), Ludvigsen Library (c), Motoring Picture Library/National Motor Museum (bc); 67: Neill Bruce Motoring Photolibrary, Peter Roberts Collection (c), Corbis, David Lees (bc); 68: Neill Bruce Motoring Photolibrary (br); 68–69: ©auto motor und sport; 69: Motoring Picture Library/National Motor Museum (bc), Nicky Wright (bl) (br); 71: Advertising Archives (cr), Corbis ©Bettmann (br); 72: GP Library (br); 75: Detroit Public Library, National Automotive History Collection (c), Ludvigsen Library (crb); 76: Neill Bruce Motoring Photolibrary, Peter Roberts Collection (bl); 79: brochure material ©British Motor Industry Heritage Trust(c) (cr) (cb) (br); 80: Corbis ©Bettmann (br); 80–81: ©auto motor und sport; 83: Motoring Picture Library/National Motor Museum (cr) (bc); 84: BMW AG Historical Archive (tr); 84–85: James Mann; 87: BMW AG Historical Archive (c) (cr) (br); 88: Ludvigsen Library (bl), Motoring Picture Library/National Motor Museum (br); 91: Neill Bruce Motoring Photolibrary, Peter Roberts Collection (bc); 93: Motoring Picture Library/National Motor Museum (br); 95: brochure material ©British Motor Industry Heritage Trust (cr) (c) (cb), Lat Photographic (br); 96: Lat Photographic: (br); 97: Lat Photographic (bl) (bc) (br); 101: GP Library (bl), Ludvigsen Library (bc), Rover Group, BMIHT, Beaulieu (br); 102: GP Library (bc); 102–103: GP Library; 103: Ace Photo Agency; Michael Woodward (cl), Motoring Picture Library/National Motor Museum (bc), Rover Group, BMIHT, Beaulieu (cr); 104: Neill Bruce Motoring Photolibrary (bl) (br), Lat Photographic (bc); 107: Neill Bruce Motoring Photolibrary, Peter Roberts Collection (br); 108–109: GP Library; 109: Corbis ©Bettmann (bl), Ronald Grant Archive, From Bullitt/Warner Brothers (br); 111: AKG London (cb), Neill Bruce Motoring Photolibrary, Peter Roberts Collection (cr); 115: Motoring Picture Library/National Motor Museum (bc); 117: Ronald Grant Archive, From April Love/Twentieth Century Fox (tr); 119: Neill Bruce

Motoring Photolibrary, Peter Roberts Collection (cr); 120: Collection Amicale Facel-Vega (bl); 123: Collection Amicale Facel-Vega (c) (cr), Lat Photographic (bc); 124: Neill Bruce Motoring Photolibrary (bl) (bc), Motoring Picture Library/National Motor Museum (br); 125: Neill Bruce Motoring Photolibrary (bl) (bc); 127: Jaguar Daimler Heritage Trust (c) (cr) (bc); 128: Neill Bruce Motoring Photolibrary, Peter Roberts Collection (bl); 131: brochure material ©British Motor Industry Heritage Trust (c) (cr) (br); 133: GP Library (tr); 135: Neill Bruce Motoring Photolibrary, Peter Roberts Collection (c), brochure material ©British Motor Industry Heritage Trust (cr) (cb) (br); 136: GP Library (bl), Ludvigsen Library (br), James Mann (bc); 139: Advertising Archives (c), Ludvigsen Library (br), James Mann (cr); 140: Archivio Adolfo Orsi (bl); 140–141: Auto Italia; 143: Ludvigsen Library (cr), Archivio Adolfo Orsi (br); 144: Giles Chapman (br), GP Library (bl); 149: Motoring Picture Library/National Motor Museum (br); 151: Motoring Picture Library/National Motor Museum (tcr); 152–153: Bob Bondurant School of High Performance Driving/Rob Beddington Collection; 153: Nissan Motor Corporation in the USA/Rob Beddington Collection (br); 155: Neill Bruce Motoring Photolibrary, Peter Roberts Collection (br), Nissan Motor Company/Rob Beddington Collection (cr); 159: Car Photo Library (bc); 161: ©auto motor und sport: (bc); 162: Motoring Picture Library/National Motor Museum (bc); 162–163: Neill Bruce Motoring Photolibrary, Peter Roberts Collection; 163: Advertising Archives (bc), Motoring Picture Library/National Motor Museum (cl); 164–165: ©auto motor und sport; 167: Archivio Storico Alfa Romeo (c); 168: Ronald Grant Archive, From Silent Movie/Twentieth Century Fox (bl); 169: Motoring Picture Library/National Motor Museum (tc); 171: Morgan Motor Company (cr), Motoring Picture Library/National Motor Museum (tl); 172: Neill Bruce Motoring Photolibrary, Peter Roberts Collection (bl); 175: British

Motor Industry Heritage Trust (c) (bc); 176: Hulton Getty Archive (bl); 179: Motoring Picture Library/National Motor Museum (c); 180: BMIHT, Advertising Archives (tr); 183: BMIHT, Advertising Archives (br), BMIHT/Motorpresse Internationale (cr); 185: Neill Bruce Motoring Photolibrary, Peter Roberts Collection (br); 187: Ludvigsen Library (bc); 188: Lat Photographic (bl) (bc) (br); 189: Daimler Chrysler Classic Archives (bl) (bc); 191: Daimler Chrysler Classic Archives (c); 195: Advertising Archives (bc); 197: ©auto motor und sport (bc), Motoring Picture Library/National Motor Museum (bl); 198–199: ©auto motor und sport; 198: MotoringPictureLibrary/National Motor Museum (or); 199: Neill Bruce Motoring Photolibrary, Peter Roberts Collection (br); 200–201: Porsche Ag; 201: Porsche Ag; 203: Porsche Ag: (cr) (c); 204: Motoring Picture Library/National Motor Museum (bl); 208: ©auto motor und sport (br), Motoring Picture Library/National Motor Museum (tl) (bl); 208–209: Auto Italia; 211: AKG London, Tony Vaccaro (cl), Neill Bruce Motoring Photolibrary, Peter Roberts Collection (crb), Motoring Picture Library/National Motor Museum (tl); 212: Car Photo Library (tl); 215: Car Photo Library (tl), Mirror Syndication International (c) (cr), ©auto motor und sport (br); 216: Lat Photographic (br); 219: Neill Bruce Motoring Photolibrary, Peter Roberts Collection (c) (cr) (br); 220: Roger Stowers; 221: BMW AG Historical Archive; 222: BMW AG Historical Archive; 223: James Mann.

Midsummer Books provided main car images, car profiles, and detail images for the following pages: 18–19, 26–27, 30–31, 38–39, 42–43, 46–47, 50–51, 74–75, 78–79, 82–83, 86–87, 94–95, 98–99, 106–07, 114–15, 118–19, 122–23, 130–31, 134–35, 146–47, 150–51, 154–55, 166–67, 170–71, 178–79, 182–83, 194–95, 202–03, 206–07, 210–11, 214–15, 218–19.